Yantra, Mantra and Tantrism: The Complete Guide

Yantra, Mantra and Tantrism: The Complete Guide

by Deepak Rana

Neepradaka Press

Published by Neepradaka Press 2012
All rights reserved.

ISBN: 978-0-9564928-3-8

Copyright © 2012 by Deepak Rana

Deepak Rana asserts the moral right to be identified as the author of this work.

All rights reserved. No part of this publication may be reproduced, stored in a retrieval system, or transmitted in any form or by any means, electronic, mechanical, photocopying, recording or otherwise, without the prior consent of the Publishers.

All names where appropiate have been changed to aliases in interests of privacy.

Acknowledgements

My thanks to the following for their valued contribution to this book.

Gopalakah Vamandaran, Meenakshi Dhandor, Jonathan Abracham, Dharmedra Suri, Prof. AshokeDhander, BasanatiKamale, Nathan Longthorn, Dr. Jheeevandhbhai Ghokula, Rameshri Bhoguna, Jharoorbhai Rana, Nagabhai Kholam Leenaben Mistry, Prof, Prakash Mehras, Rabeenaben Lekhani, Dr.Beelal Oja, Paul Rodrigrez Arakneranjan Bherunelam, Silveriaaum Bhookhi, Balaram Jhanuswar, NatraveelaJeevansham, Dr. Kailash Nagar, Neelisha Devi, Harish Patel PhoolamParankeedash, RajubhaiKapilesah, Khalsijen Desai, Teanamunim Rana, Dr.John B. Bolugra, Carlos Nadeem, Dr.Baljit Singh, LalderInduja, Dr. Amitabh Battchan, Vijay Veerulal

Also available from Neepradaka Press

The Secret Power of Lists

Contents

Foreword	15
Author/Editor Preface	19
Introduction	23
Part 1: Tantra, Yantra and the Vedic Texts	27
The Veda's	30
Post-Vedic texts: Smriti	32
Other Important Poems	
The Tantric Texts	35
Part 2: Yantra for the Tantric	47
Aims of the Tantric	48
The Yantra and Tantrism	49
Yantra Charging	51
Tantric Sex	51
Creation of Yantra	56
Yogic Practice	58
Use of Breath	61
Hand Gestures	63
The Use's of Yantra	64
The Categories or types of Yantra	65
Zakti Mani	69
Placement of Yantra	72
Materials used for the Yantra	74
Writing Instrument for Yantra	78
Time and Place	78
Drawing of Yantra	81
Triangles	82

Quantum world, sacred geometry & Yantra	83
Fibonacci Sequence	84
Use of Mantra	86
Tantric Mantra	92
Yantra Mantra and Hemispherical synchronisation	93
Part 3: Tantrism and Yantra in Practice	97
Introduction	98
Specific Use's of Yantra	99
Part 4: Obtaining a Yantra	121
Introduction	122
Purchasing from the internet	126
India	127
Location Maps	135
Part 5: Yantra Images	141
References	187
Appendix: Websites	195
Final Word	199

Foreword

Yantra

Dr. Jeevan Ghoswami: Chairman: South Indian Vedic Consciousness Movement. Editor for 'Sanskrit Times', 'Hinduism Today & Tomorrow', and regular contributor to a range of Indian newspapers and journals.

I am very pleased to endorse this outstanding work. For the first time we are presented with a thoroughly researched work around the subject of Yantra's, especially within Tantric use which a lot of works have not explored in great depth. In particular it places this very complex topic within context of the ancient Vedic and Tantric texts in an understandable way. The types and categories of Yantra are clearly explained and a lot of academics will find this extremely useful for their own research. Here, also for the first time are mathematical concepts applied to the drawing of some Yantra which amalgamates mathematics and quantum physics to provide an intriguing insight into the world of Yantra. It reaffirms the advanced knowledge that is described in the Veda's and subsequently passed down through generations of Hindu's.

I am proud of this rich source of knowledge and its deep spiritual essence that has survived for thousands of years and which can benefit mankind greatly. May this work enlighten others as it as done for me and I encourage everyone to share it. I for one have already recommended its use within Sanskrit courses delivered in Indian colleges and Universities, and look forward to it being a set text in India and abroad.

Author/Editor Preface

Yantra

Originally scheduled for publication in early 2011, this work has taken longer than anticipated. It is likely the publication would have been further delayed had it not been for the tireless work of the contributors to ensure that the 2012 deadline could be met. An immense work such as this also requires an understanding publisher and Neepradaka Press have been kind in this regard.

When so many contributors from various locations across the world are involved in a project, it is both a costly and time consuming task to ensure communications are maintained. This has been problematic in some cases due to the very locations that some contributors have journeyed to, and sometimes months have passed before any news has been heard from them. Sometimes workloads, or other projects have placed great demands, and some have had to reluctantly give up their work on this project. So again, time(sometimes months), has been taken to find alternative researchers to replace those who have left. However the positive outcome of this has meant the provision of more time for researchers to go further in their explorations and to seek out new sources of information. This has led to some interesting, and previously unpublished information about Yantra and Tantrism, and in turn greatly enhanced the value of this work. As a writer and editor of this work it has been a challenging task to bring together the numerous reports, images, photographs, maps, and diagrams into a coherent piece of work. This coupled with audio and video files submitted for which the contributors did not have the time or the facilities to go through to extract relevant information. I do feel I have managed to bring everything together in this book and that nothing of vital importance has been left out. First, second, and third drafts were circulated to all contributors as well as other scholars, and the feedback has been positive. In fact a high volume of pre-orders were already in place towards the end of 2011 on the strength of the earlier drafts. So it is with confidence that I say that everyone will find value in this work and hope it will lead to people wanting to explore further ancient Vedic knowledge.

Introduction

Many texts published in English both in India and elsewhere on the subject of Yantra have either lacked essential information, or have provided inaccurate information. This has been due to many reasons such as lack of research and cross referencing of sources, and/or misinformation passed on in good faith and not double checked. Another reason has been the particular bias of an author with leanings to a particular branch of Tantrism, and therefore knows little else of the practices which take place within other Tantric sects.

This book seeks to correct the inaccurate information that has been provided in other works to date on the subject of Yantra. The information has been thoroughly researched using a number of historical sources as well as first hand research. First hand research has come from those who either practice Tantrism itself, or whose families have practised it and are able to provide reliable and accurate information. In addition, this has included discussions with those who have a great deal of knowledge gained either professionally or otherwise. This has allowed extensive cross referencing and further reinforces the accuracy of the information.

There is also, for the first time, discussion of the science of Yantra's and in particular recent work within quantum physics, which will be of special value to academic researchers. The subject of Yantra and Tantric practise is a complex one and many works have fallen in to the trap of using complex language which has only confused the reader. This book has tried as much as possible to use clear language to explain the subject in an easy to understand way.

For many non-academic readers, their interest in Yantra has been arrived at because they have been offered Yantra for sale, or they have heard about the benefits of Yantra and have wished to make a purchase for their own use. It is the case that a lot of Yantra on sale are of dubious quality and lack any beneficial power. By understanding what Yantra are, and how they are created, the reader will be able to understand the rarity of powerful Yantra's and why it is not just a matter of buying off the shelf Yantra. Genuine Yantra are personalised according to Vedic principles and techniques which are described in this book. For those wishing to purchase such Yantra, details are provided on possible places to go and how to check authenticity.

This book is divided in to three parts; Part 1 looks at the history of Yantra by first placing the subject within the context of the Vedic texts (and Tantrism). It explores how and why Yantra are a major element in Tantric practice. Part 2 expands on Tantrism and provides further detail on Yantra, such as particular categories of Yantra and specific uses within Tantra. There is discussion on the materials used when creating a Yantra as well as exploration of mathematical concepts behind some of the Yantra designs. This chapter also discusses Mantra. Mantra are always used as part of the creation and use of Yantra. Mantra is explained in relation to scientific theory on the nature and effect of sound waves. Part 4 of this book discusses obtaining Yantra. This will help anyone to discover how they can obtain genuine powerful Yantra, and this is the part of the book that has taken the greatest amount of time and research to complete. The final part of the book provides images of genuine Yantra, most of which have been scanned from the original article.

PART 1

Tantra, Yantra and the Vedic texts

Yantra

Introduction

One cannot begin to discuss Yantra without relating it to Hinduism and it's various texts. Tantrism and the use of Yantra are all born out from these ancient Vedic texts. It is these ancient Vedic texts where we must thus begin our discussion of Yantra.

The literature of Hindu texts has predominately been written in the Sanskrit language and these sacred Vedic texts are known either as Shruti (revelation texts), stemming from that which has been divinely revealed, and Smriti, that which is of human origin. Although, one must understand that some texts are an amalgamation of both, and thus one cannot easily suggest that a text is one or the other. However, this categorization is still used widely by academics and has proven to be quite useful in certain contexts. What makes up Hindu religious texts are derived from hymns(which enabled them to be easily remembered and recited), and were passed down from generation to generation, either within families, or through guru disciple relationships. Although written language did exist it was not used extensively at first. However when faced with the problems of invasions by the muslims, the writing down of texts became a necessity. Over time other texts were also added which resulted in a wide body of sacred texts now described as the Vedas. Further texts continued to be added to further explain, develop and highlight aspects of the original Vedic texts. A brief overview of the texts will be provided here, which will help to understand the vast range of topics that the Veda's cover and explain how Tantric texts (and use of Yantra) fit within the Veda's.

The Veda's

The list of oldest Vedic texts can be seen to be made up of four parts, or collections: Rig-veda, Sama-veda, Yajur-veda, and Atharava-veda. These four parts also include with them other distinctive texts which are given their own names. These four parts are explained in turn.

Rigveda

These are a collection of over a thousand hymns or Mantras and divided in to ten books called Mandalas. Essentially it is composed of hymns praising various Gods and Goddesses, and divine beings. The Rigveda has been the most difficult and complex work to study, not only in current times but also in ancient times. In fact, Yaska, a Sanskrit grammarian, sought to develop a glossary of words in the Rigveda which had lost their meanings, and which for many had become words spoken without any understanding of their meanings. Within the Rigveda we have the Aitareya-Asvalayana Brahmanas, the Aitareya Kausitaki Aranyakas, and the Aitareya Kausitaki Upanishads.

Samaveda

A collection of hymns from the original Rigveda, but with some new ones added. Priests generally chanted hymns from the Samaveda and included particular tunes that had to be sung using the correct pitch. Within this is included the Tandya Sadvimsa Brahmanas, and the Kena Chandogya Upanishads.

Yajurveda

These were texts which helped priests follow the rituals and ceremonies described in the Rigveda. It provides instructions on how altar's should be constructed for the rituals described. We also find here two divisions of rituals, black and white. The black division provides deeper explanations of the meaning behind some of the rituals and sacrifices which are performed. This includes the Taittiriya Satapatha Brahmanas, the Brhadaranyaka Taittiriya Aranyakas, and the Taittiriya Isa Katha Upanishads.

Atharavaveda

The Atharaveda's has been purported by some scholars to have been composed by families of priests that were known as Atharvans. Atharaveda is composed of magic spells, hymns and rituals, and differs from the Vedas which preceded it, in that they are based on everyday religious ideas rather than the lives of Gods. There are also a hundred and fourteen hymns which speak of the treatment of diseases and it is this from which we have the science of Ayurveda which is described later in this chapter.

Sutras

Many scholars have made a mistake in creating a 'Sutra' category when discussing Vedic texts. This is incorrect and will become apparent when we understand what the word Sutra refers to. Sutra is a collection or block of a particular idea which can be composed of a number of lines, and are written in such a way to enable it to be easily remembered. Therefore we can actually find Sutra's throughout the Vedic texts, and scholars have separated particular ones out when discussing certain ideas. Sutras have thus been mentioned here as an aid to understanding.

Post-Vedic texts: Smriti

We now turn our attention to a large number of texts which are termed as Smriti. Although not considered to be revealed texts, they have been authored by significant individuals throughout India's past. These texts are described in the following pages.

<u>Puranas</u>
The Puranas comprise a vast bank of medieval literature

made up of stories and allegory. Eighteen are considered Mahapurana (great) purana, and are authoritative references on Gods, Goddesses, religious rites and holy places in the world (of which most are in the Indian subcontinent).

These eighteen puranas are made up of six Vaisnava (Sattva) Puranas, six Saiva (rajasa) Purana, and six Brahma (tamasa) Puranas. There are 18 Upapauranas.

Dharmasastras (codes of law)
These are texts relating to all processes and thoughts regarding methods of living within society (codes of conduct), and the operation of civil and criminal law, and atonement/punishment

Tevaramsaivite hymns
Composed around 1400-1200 years ago by three Tamil composers.

DivyaPrabandha Vaishnavite hymns
Divine collection of four thousand verses originally composed before 8th century AD, by twelve poet saints (alvars), and was subsequently compiled in its present form by Nathamunigal during the 9th and 10th centuries. The work is the beginning of the canonization of the twelve Vaishnava poet saints, and these hymns are still sung extensively today. These works were thought to have been lost, however Nathamunigal

was able to track them down and perform the mammoth task of organising them in the form of an anthology. The DivyaPrabandha sings the praise of SrimanNarayana (or Vishnu) and his many forms. The Alvars sung these songs at various sacred shrines and these shrines are known as the DivyaDesams.

In South India especially, in Tamil Nadu, the DivyaPrabhandha is considered as equal to the Vedas, hence the term Dravida Veda is often applied. In many temples, such as in Srirangam, the chanting of the DivyaPrabhandham forms a major part of the daily service. Prominent among the four thousand verses are the one thousand plus verses known as the ThiruVaaymozhi, composed by Kaari lMaaran Sadagopan of ThirukKurugoor.

Other Important Poems

Other important poems include Ramcharitmanas of Tulsidas, which is an epic poem based on the Ramayana. The Gita Govinda of Jayadeva, is a religious song about the divine love of Krishna and his consort Radha. There are Ramanujacharya's nine books including 'Sri Bhasya' Madhvacharya's commentaries, and the Devi Mahatmya, which are the tales of Devi, the mother goddess, in her many forms as Shakti, Durga, Parvati, etc.

Ayurveda

This deals with a large body of texts which concern itself with all aspects of health. It has its basis in the Atharaveda.

Vedangas

The Vedangas can be described both as texts, and as guides to texts, and are concerned primarily with the study and understanding of the Veda's. They can be split into particular areas of study which are as follows:

Siksa: This includes phonetics, ways of speaking, tone, pitch, and all such related aspects.
Chandas: Rhythmic structure of verses (metre)
Vyakarana: Grammar
Nirukta: History of words and meaning (etymology)
Jyotisa: Astronomical science and the calendar
Kalpa: Concerned with rituals

The Tantric texts

The Tantric texts have posed a problem for those trying to classify them into something that can be understood coherently and to be able to make sense of both the origin and development of Tantrism.
Most researchers begin with the three schools of thought,

Vaisnavas, Saivas and the Saktas. Other scholars look to classifying texts as Agama and Nigama. The difference being that Agama involves texts describing Parvati, asking questions of her teacher Siva, whilst Nigama is the opposite. Then we have Tantra using the place of origin as a classification system, such as Visnuakranta, Rathakranta and Gajakranta.
We also have a classification based upon the initial letters of mantra's. These are Kadi, Hadi and Sadi. Then we have classifications based on the five faces of Siva. Each face is said to have produced ten Agamas; Kamika, Yogaja, Cintya, Mukuta, Amsuman, Dipta, Sahastra, Ajita, Suprabheda and Ajita. Following from these are further texts leading to eighteen Raudra Agamas. Recent scholarly works have distilled Tantric works into four categories of work; Agama, Damara, Yamala, and Tantra.

Some scholars have avoided the categorization altogether and instead have identified significant elements within Tantric works. These are as follows:

(a) Vidya: Knowledge both philosophical and mystical.
(b) Yoga: Control of the mind in particular to acquire special powers.
(c) Kriya: Creation of idols and temples and appropriate consecration.
(d) Siddhi: Instructions for rites, festivals.

Yantra

As can be seen it is a difficult task to fully comprehend the breath and complexity of the varieties of Tantric texts, and the branches of Tantrism that have evolved from them.

For example there is the Kaulism which evolved to ritual devotion to particular goddess's. In fact a lot of Tantrism involves working with feminine energy (the Kundalini is conceptualized as feminine energy), and therefore one can find devotion to quite a variety of Goddess's within Tantric practice. Another school of thought is that of Srividya school which attempted to create some kind of structure and philosophical explanations for the practices within the Tantric system.

It is important to note that Tantra can be viewed in the most general sense or in a rather more restricted application. In its most general definition, Tantra can actually encompass the practices, Mantras and rituals as described in any of the Hindu sacred texts. In the most restrictive use of the term it is used to describe those rituals, practices and Mantras which are not derived from the Veda's, but specifically from the Tantric texts that was just described. This explains some of the confusion with both academics and laypersons who take on the restrictive meaning of the term, and dismiss Tantra to be something that stands apart from all the other Vedic texts. Another source of confusion is that some texts, although labelled as Tantric are not, and some texts which are Tantric in nature are not labelled as such. It is thus down to a lot of research, and the skills of readers, translators and Vedic historians, which has assisted with bringing Tantrism to a better understanding. To confuse matters further the word Tantra itself has been debated as to the original source of the word. For example Tanu to mean 'body' in Sanskrit has a similarity to the word 'Tantra', and thus it is suggested that this is how the word Tantra has come about, as Tantra involves the body (in terms of Yogic postures). Another source is said to be from the word 'Tantri' which means 'to explain', and yet another source is the word 'Tan' to mean 'spread', such as to spread knowledge.

Fear has also played a part in misunderstanding. For example, some of the strange behaviours displayed by some Tantrics (those who follow the extremes along the Tantric continuum), can appear incomprehensible and very frightening. Confusion and fear has thus left a lot of misunderstanding and incorrect publications that tell little of the full story of what Tantra is, and what it isn't. Those who observe Tantric tradition can just like many other aspects and facets of Hinduism, follow Tantrism's along a continuum of moderate to extreme practice.

Tantrism involves a great deal of ritualised practice. Ritualised, in that every use of sounds (Mantras), gestures, particular bodily movements(yoga), breathing and concentrated meditation, require particular rituals. Yantra are used as an essential part of this package of ritualised practise, and the creation of them, similarly, requires a particular set of rituals and steps. These have, over time been refined, developed and shared in order to maximise their effectiveness in Tantric practise. They thus are an important tool used in Tantric practice. They remained used in this way for a long time, but gradually some Yantra began to be seen in homes and worn by people who did not themselves follow Tantric practices. How could this have come about? Well it was common in ancient times as it is now for the common man and woman to seek advice and blessings from holy people. The kind of help sought in those times is likely to have been the same as today, such as help with relationships, and material assistance, whether it be more land then or a new house today. These holy people who followed Tantric practice's would have therefore prescribed certain rituals and provided particular mantra, and Yantra to help those who did not themselves follow Tantrism.

It must be understood that the use of Yantra did not just come about within the Tantric tradition but is mentioned in much earlier Hindu texts which do not on the face of it appear to relate to Tantrism. For example if one looks at the texts relating to architecture one can see a lot of Yantra type designs because of the very fact that Yantra shapes and designs were believed to have 'power', and be able to harness energy. There is some research to suggest Yantra were in use on a planetary scale.

Today temples are seen as places to go and worship God

and conduct ceremonies and rituals. However they were never built for God worship. Temples were in fact places to go and sit alone in quiet contemplation and meditation, and were built according to Vedic principles and according to Yantra designs. This provided such temples the necessary energy and vibration to enhance and support all those who came to the temple. In addition to being designed around Yantra designs, these temples would in addition have certain Yantra placed within their foundations, and some even had Yantra's placed within temple walls. Images on pages 43 to 44 are examples of ancient temples built according to Yantra designs. Image on page 45 is an example of a Yantra kept within a home temple.

Yantra

Yantra

PART 2
Yantra for the Tantric

Part one described how Yantra have been mentioned in the earliest Vedic texts, and an important tool within the Tantric tradition. This part of the book will discuss Tantrism further, and further expand on Yantra.

Aims of the Tantric

Depending on the particular tradition followed, the aims of the person practicing Tantrism can be varied. It can include the development of special powers with the aim of eventual liberation. For others the aim may be to develop control of oneself, and of the outer material world. Such powers are well documented in literature such as the ability to withstand extremes of temperature, low oxygen levels and the ability to sustain life for months without food or water. The initiation of a person into the Tantric tradition can be undertaken by the family of the person (if the rest of the family or certain members of the family are following a Tantric path). For others, they will be on a spiritual journey which will bring them to someone who can initiate them into Tantrism. The Tantric Guru is an important role in itself and the qualities of a Guru are described in the Paranandasutra (56, 63), and the Mahanirvana (verses 201-202).

The initiation requires a great deal of dedication on the part of the initiate, and prepares him for the development of his mind and body. He also begins to learn about the nature of Yantra and Mantra. The initiation consists of the rebirth via the death and transmutation of the initiate, and can also involve other types of initiation which can take place over a number of days, and involves ceremony and rituals to be undertaken, along with the use of Mantra and Yantra. The concept of rebirth is related to the concept of upanayana where one attains a second birth which is spiritual, as opposed to a physical one. This is also linked in with the eclipse which is favoured as the day for initiation. The eclipse signifies the death of the sun or moon and its rebirth as it emerges.

Depending on the particular school of Tantrism, the materials and ceremonies will vary. For example the use of 'forbidden' items may be used such as wine, meat, eggs, fish for those Tantric traditions which follow the left hand path of Tantrism. This can also involve various sexual activity as part of the initiation ritual. Towards the end of the ceremony the initiate is imparted a personal secret Mantra, along with a new name.

The Yantra and Tantrism

The Tantric Yantra (once created according to specific principles) is both a physical object and a non-physical object incorporating specific levels of life. If one takes the example of a rose, one can see immediately its physical structure and colour properties. On the secondary level we can associate the rose with love or a number of other associations. Then, on a deeper level there are the atomic structures which are unseen which give rise to the physical rose. Deeper still is the non-physical subtle energy level of the rose, which vibrates at a particular set of frequencies, and without which the rose would not give rise to the object we recognise as a rose. The Yantra therefore provides a doorway to both represent, as well as act upon all levels of the physical and non-physical world (the seen and the unseen aspects of life). When created according to set principles, and energised with the Tantric abilities of a practising Tantric, the Yantra becomes a powerful tool to bring about effects in the material and non-material world (including the energy centres of the body chakra's). In addition the sound (Mantra), sometimes written on the Yantra itself also forms part of the Yantra. Tantric rituals make a lot of use of sounds/Mantras, and these sounds themselves are not just physical changes in the air but also provide a way of working with particular energies that are affected by sound vibrations. Sound is just another form of energy and it is these particular sounds which create particular energies. The origins of Mantras have been revealed to those undertaking meditative practice and have then been described in Vedic texts. Furthermore some Mantras have never been written down but passed on through guru disciple relationships. Mantra can be categorised as hot or cold Mantra's, and will relate to the ritual being carried out and the purpose of that ritual. Further information about Mantra can be found on page 86.

Yantra Charging

The aim of the charging process is so that the Yantra becomes 'alive', and be able to become an energy unit which can harness energies in accordance to the type of Yantra required. First begins a process of purification of the Tantric performing the charging process, followed by the invocation of the specific energies required. These energies are represented by specific divinities, with the aim of bringing such energies into the Tantric and thereafter transferred into the Yantra. The transference process then is performed, and can involve various methods, for example the use of breath force via yogic breathing, Mantra recitals, and various hand gestures. Throughout the Yantra charging process there may be involved the use of various materials such as holy water, blood, semen,, breast milk, urine, honey etc.

Once a Yantra has been charged it is said to be alive and therefore also requires daily puja worship, (although this is not the case with all Yantra).

Tantric sex

A popular topic for many in the Western world. The first time many would have heard the word 'Tantric', is in relation to sexual activity.

There has been a lot of misunderstanding and confusion relating to Tantric sex, mainly because the focus has been upon the physical activity itself rather than the spiritual aspects which is the essential component, and the reason for the various practices involved. Within Tantrism the use of various sexual activity forms just one of the many rituals and practices in Tantrism, and it is within this context one must seek to understand it.

Take for example the popularised aspect in the West regarding the use of Tantric sex to increase the length and strength of the orgasmic experience. Through proper yogic training this is possible, but the aim is not the physical orgasmic experience itself but the associated mental and psychical experience which is linked in with the concept of the chakra (or energy centres within the body). The sexual union of male and female is also ritualised and intercourse and various positions are used as part of Tantric practice. In general the use of Tantric sex usually takes place within a group, although some practices can be undertaken by a couple. This is often described as a Circle Puja or Cakrapuja, and its secrets are to be kept and not disclosed (Kularnava xi, 79, 84, 85).

Generally in such rituals the male does not discharge any semen, although if this occurs accidently, then the semen is spread on the forehead for absorption of power (Kalivilasa-tantra x, 20-21). For women there is no restriction on holding back on the orgasmic experience, and is in fact nurtured in order that beneficial secretions are released from within the vagina. Such secretions are collected, added to water and drunk as part of the rituals. Another way to absorb the power of the vaginal secretions, is via the insertion of the penis by the male who has to be trained in absorbing the power of these secretions. Within these Tantric sexual practices are the aims to control and transform bodily energies (and where the concept of the chakra's and energy channels comes in). Through the skilled use of Tantric sexual practice and ritual, the sexual act becomes a vehicle for spiritual progress. This progress is not instant but can take place over many years, and is by no means a straight path. Some Tantrics are succumbed by the various powers that come as part of the energisation processes and lose their way.

Some of these powers in relation to Tantric sex is being able to cause instant sexual arousals within females or males, simply by a gaze or a simple touch on the hand. One of the researchers of this book described her experience on visiting one Tantric who had developed particular Tantric powers to a high degree.

'I asked if he would be able to demonstrate some of the Tantric powers he had developed. He asked my permission to touch my hand and so I offered it to him palm downwards. With one hand he touched the middle of the top of my hand and I felt like warm water was being poured over it. It was a nice sensation, and then I felt the sensation spread down up arm and I felt a great sense of physical arousal. I felt my body begin to vibrate and I could not help but move my body as waves and waves of pleasure filled me'.

The following is the first hand account of a Tantric sexual partner (translated).

'Certain times of the month we will focus on using our combined energies to excite these energies and vibrate them to their highest point. It is something that must be practiced on a regular basis which allows us to develop a mastery of them. The control of energies is the most difficult aspect of our work…I have been given knowledge of certain physical processes which I practise when I am with my partner. For example the internal massage is one process which is used to begin a stoking of both our energies. This involves the internal control of my Yoni musculature when the phallus is rested within it'.

Sometimes groups of male and female Tantrics will come together to combine energies. The following account is from a practicing Tantric (translated).

'There are one or two times within the year which is very special. Those days are very powerful and a Tantric is able to harness more energy in order to help his or her development.

A few days before the special day itself we are able to sense the increasing energies around us and we enter states of meditation in preparation for the day. These mediation periods allow us to prepare our minds and bodies for the day to come, and also involves the consumption of specially prepared foods which include animal and vegetable items. In this time we take part in the 'milking' which is the stoking of physical desire up to its highest points but not to the point of total release. This can involve massage, and the use of Tantric devices. For example I have used a wooden ball upon which I sit and thereby stimulate my base chakra. When the day comes we form small groups. These can be a mix of female and males, or completely made up of one sex, there is no strict rule on this. In these groups we engage in all physical sexual activity involving our bodies and our minds with the aim to harness and develop our energies. Our group as a whole becomes highly energised and extremely powerful. I have seen for myself the ability for groups to levitate a few feet from the ground, to lift heavy rocks, to cause the body to emit light from the eyes and the ability to see beings from other dimensions and worlds. This sexual power is evident in all human beings. In the orgasmic experience, all humans are able to glimpse momentarily an absolute bliss. For many in the world this is probably the only time when they will be able to have such a mystical experience. This is the reason why all humans yearn to experience such orgasmic states over and over again'.

Another account explains the role of massage:

'Massage is an effective way to start the flow of energy. This has been labelled by some as 'tantric massage', but this is not specifically a tantric tool. Ancient texts speak of massage for healing, for conditioning of the body, and even for massage of animals for health. The aim of massage in tantric practice is to begin to move the energy, and also to serve to eliminate negative chemical toxins which may cause problems in our practice. In most cases this massage takes place between two people, male and female. Various positions are also involved as not just the hands but other parts of the body are used for the massage. For example the heel, nose, knee are all utilised for massage'.

Creation of Yantra's

The person who creates a Yantra will be someone who has the knowledge and experience of Tantric practice and who lives their life within this traditional field. Such people will have been indoctrinated into such work as part of family tradition, and it is common to find families in India who can trace back many generations of individuals within the family who made Tantric practice a major part of their life and work. For example one family called the Karshikania can trace creation of Yantra for kings during the Ashoka, and the Gupta era which followed it.

Yantra   57

There are also those who have renounced family and taken on singular paths in order for self-realisation. These individuals may have taken on a particular Tantric school of thought and may be found offering services such as Yantra creation (often part of a package of help) for all those that seek it.

Now it is clear that there are those in India, such as temple priests, and modern day guru's who create Yantra for all of lifes various problems and ailments. However it must be understood that the creation of these Yantra may not have any beneficial effects simply because they have not been created correctly. As can be deduced above (and from the information later in this book), few have the dedication and commitment to follow the Tantric path, or come from a family where tantrism has been within a family for generations. So what we are offered by such temple priests, Guru's, and market sellers, are products which may have been created incorrectly, or Yantra created from a limited amount of knowledge which brings little or no benefit, or in some cases negative effects.

Yogic Practice

Regular yogic practices are an important element in the life of someone following a Tantric path. One of the aims of yogic practice is for the Kundalaini (a coiled energy force that resides within the base of the spine), to ascend to its highest ultimate point, and to remain there. As the energy force rises it activates the chakra's (energy centres) along its path, leading to an awakening of that chakra and is associated with various mystical experiences. Chakra's are centres of energy which number seven in total and sit at various points along the spine, and then up towards the brain.

The awakening of each of these chakra's is a gradual process that can take many years as the kundalini ascends. Other yogic practices involve a branch of yoga known as hatha yoga which is what many in the West will think of when asked to describe what yoga is. In some Tantric traditions the ball of energy within the base of the spine is visualised as a Goddess which must be unified with the male energy to achieve the ultimate balance on the physical and cosmic level. Some of the practices associated with such Kundalini awakening include the ritual use of sexual energy (Tantric sex described earlier). Hatha yoga is the use of physical bodily movements to purify and condition the body and in turn assist with the other yogic practices described.

Yantra

The diagram scanned from an early metal plate illustrates where the Chakra's can be pinpointed on the human body. The chart provides further exposition of the chakra's.

Chakra Name	Description
Sahasra dala Kamala	This lies just above the head. It is seen as a thousand petal lotus comprising of 50 letters repeated twenty times.
Ajna Chakra	This lies in what is commonly referred to as the third-eye. It is seen as two white petals bearing two letters.
Visudha Chakra	Known as the throat Chakra due to its position. It is seen as 16 grey petals on which are written ten letters in red.
Anahata Chakra	Known as the heart chakra due to its placement.. It is said to be where the seat of the soul lies. It is seen as twelve pink petals. This is also termed as Atma-Ram and can sometimes be seen after death as an orb.
Manipuraka Chakra	Situated where the navel is, and sometimes referred to as the seat of fire.

Swadhistana Chakra	This lies at the heart of the reproduction organs, and visualised as a light red chakra.
Mooladhara Chakra	Below the above Chakra at the very seat of the spine between the anus and the base of the penis, or the start of the outer vaginal lips. This is seen as a much deeper blood like colour.

Use of Breath

Breath work has behind it a large body of texts which aim to describe the importance of breath and how to utilise it within spiritual work. Most people breath without any conscious thought, whilst those undergoing a spiritual path will always be consciously breathing. This will for example involve the speed at which air is taken into the body, to how it is exhaled. Here is an account of the importance of breathing from a Tantric:

'Every state affects our breathing. Notice that when you are angry, your breathing changes. Notice when a painful, shocking event occurs and how we stop our breathing. See how certain feelings within us can be linked to negativity, and how we limit our breath in order to numb or to press down feelings to prevent them from coming out. This is not good for feelings must be expressed not pressed down using the power of breath. If we use breath in this way, we eventually prevent positive feelings and joy being expressed to the world. We prevent past negativity from being expressed and dealt with, and therefore events from our past will continue to affect our present, and our future. Therefore breath must be used positively, so as to free deeply held feelings and therefore to allow us to live good lives. In Tantric practice we use breath to free ourselves from past negative hurts and feelings. We use breath to ensure we do not get pulled back in to our past lives. We use breath to manipulate the energies in our bodies and to work with our chakra's. Even those who do not work within tantrism will find benefit in working consciously with breath'.

Here is another account which talks specifically about nostril breathing:

'The way we intake breath from the nostrils is very important. The Ida and Pinala are directly related to the left and right nostril. By closing one nostril we activate the Ida or Pingala. Most people are not aware that throughout the day, the intake of air from each nostril is never equal. There is a dominance of one nostril for a short time, and then the role is reversed and the other nostril will be dominant. This is in tune with the way we take in energy, and by focusing on the intake of air we are able to control the energy which is manifested'.

Hand Gestures

There are nine gestures that scholars have identified as used within Tantric practice as part of rituals and worship. These are detailed in the following chart.

Avahana	Folding of both hand, into which articles are placed.
Stapani	Folding of hands reversed.
Sannidhapana	Two joined fists with thumbs pointing to the sky
Sannirpdhani	Two joined fists with thumbs enclosed within
Sammukhikarani	Two closed fists raised to the sky
Sakalikriti	Use of one hand to paint the many limbs on a deity
Avagunthana	Fingers folded down and waved around an article
Dhenu	Intertwining of each finger to fingers of the other hand
Mahamudra	Intertwining of thumbs of both hands, fingers held straight

The Uses's of Yantra

Once the use of a Yantra is identified, it then provides guidance on the particular set of rituals and practice needed to create that Yantra. In addition, if the use is for a particular person then that persons astrological details must also be taken into account. The reason being that the effects of a Yantra can be enhanced or diminished based on the placement of planets during the time of birth.

The main uses of Yantra are described in the table on the next page.

1	To bring a person, animal, deity under one's control (VashiKaron). In ancient times animals were extensively used for a lot of work and thus if an animal could be brought under better control then this would greatly help in carrying out work.
2	To cure diseases and warding off the negative influences of passed on souls, and the negative influences of planets (Shanti Karan)
3	To stop or prevent plans of others causing harm (Stambhan).
4	To cause animosity between two people (Videshan).
5	To cause distractions and deflections so that a person forgets about their own home or family and breaks all associations with what they are familiar with (Uchattan).
6	To cause a persons death (Maran)

The categories or types of Yantra

A lot of works on Yantra have focused on discussing only one type of Yantra- that which is inscribed on to a copper plate. However that is just one category of Yantra and others are described in the chart on the next page.

Earth Yantra
These are so termed because they are created from the materials of the earth. The Sanskrit word for this type is BhooPrishth, and they can be raised or carved out.
Mountain Yantra
These types are shaped like a mountain, and in Sanskrit are termed MeruPrishth. There are some interesting geological surveys which point to some mountains as being man-made and it is possible to suggest that these may have been 'mountain Yantra's'

Patel Yantra.
This is an inversion of the mountain yantra.
Cut Yantra.
These are yantra's which are cut and are termed MeruParastar.
Tortoise Yantra.
These will typically have a rectangle as the base with the tortoise on the top, or sometimes a tortoise will have a mountain yantra on its back. This is also termed the Kurma Yantra, named after the second incarnation of Visnu. This type is quite rare, and examples of these are hard to locate in India. Similarly it is extremely rare to find anyone who can correctly create one due to its very difficulty. See images on Page 67-68.

Yantra

Yantra

Zakti Mani

There is one type of Yantra which has been chosen to be added as a separate category of Yantra, and that is of Zaktimani. It is unlikely to have been mentioned in any previous works due to its rare quality and because there are only two places in India where large scale examples of this type of Yantra exist. Another reason is that only in the past two years have manuscripts been translated which have described Zaktimani.

There are only a handful of families in India which possess the smaller examples of Zaktimani, and only a few of these actually know the name of what they simply term as a 'religious artefact', and which has been in the family for generations. Research also revealed the difficulty in locating those who still create Zaktimani, and this again provides the reason why Zaktimani are not widely known about.

Zaktimani are essentially a matrix of materials fused together using heat of a 'holy fire' and the recitation of particular Mantra. These materials comprise of a copper plated Yantra specifically created for this purpose, a mix of other metals, and some precious or semi-precious stones. The creation is a long and complicated process, and can easily take up to six months to create, which is why the other types of Yantra have succeeded in use and popularity, whilst Zaktimani have all but disappeared from everyday creation and use. It is unfortunate as Zaktimani have been reported to have extremely powerful effects. This was tested out using two samples of Zaktimani that had been kindly donated for the task. The Zaktimani were tested in a variety of ways over eight months utilising scientific methods to ensure accuracy.

Effect on nature

Rose experiment
Two small rose plants were purchased from the same supplier and then transported to two separate houses in the same street. Temperature, light levels and humidity were all measured and maintained to ensure both roses were in similar environments. The Zaktimani was placed next to rose 1, and no watering was applied to the roses for one month and effects were recorded by an independent observer.

It was clear after a week that Rose 2 was suffering from ill-effects. The petals were noted as losing their colour and turning brown. In week 2, Rose 1 maintained its petals, whilst Rose 2 began to lose its leaves. After the month long experiment was over, water was provided to each of the roses, and observed for a further three weeks. Rose 1 remained in a untarnished state, and began to bloom again, whilst Rose 2 began to dry up and deteriorate.

Future research has been planned, and several universities have mentioned interest in conducting vigorous scientific studies using Zakti-Mani.

Placement of Yantra

Depending on the type of Yantra that is created, a Yantra can either be worn, kept in temples (for worship), or kept in the home. This will of course be determined by the category of use for the Yantra mentioned in the preceding pages.

The placement of Yantra are described in the following table.

Chakra Yantra. These are specifically created for assistance in the awakening of the different chakras in the body, and are termed Shariryantra. In Tantric rituals, they are placed on chakra points, and will incorporate specific stones such as amethyst and lapis lazuli.
Worn Yantra's. Created for an individual person to bring about particular benefits and worn on the body such as in a ring, or tied around body parts such as neck, arms or legs. The wearing of Yantra are described in Tantrarajatantra, Patala 8, verses 30-32.
Foundation Yantra. Also termed Aasanyantra and are placed within the foundation of homes, temples, deity's or places of business to bring about beneficial effects.

Yantra

Group Yantra.
This type of Yantra is something that is created using nine people, and falls under the category of an earth Yantra. The people themselves become the Yantra. Each person recites particular Mantra's, along with rituals whilst sat in the particular Yantra formation. Due to its nature, it is a temporary Yantra and takes place at a Holy, sacred location.

Worship Yantra.
These are used during particular worship in temples or homes, and are often temporary (drawn using soluble coloured powders).

Chaatyantra- (to mean 'shade').
Such Yantra are kept under a hat, cap, or turban.

Darshannyantra
These are Yantra which are to be 'seen' and in doing so the viewer is provided beneficial energy. These also include Yantra that are meant to be visited by large numbers of people, and thus are installed in temples. Appropriate Mantra are recited to enhance beneficial effects. This category also includes Yantra's which are kept within a house to bring benefits to all those who reside there.

Materials used for the Yantra

It is common to see a lot of Yantra made from copper offered in shops and marketplaces around the world. In general these will be non-genuine, mass market Yantra (with no Vedic principles utilised in their creation). Copper, being an easy and plentiful material to work with, offers greater profits when used to create such Yantra. That is not to say that genuine Yantra are not created using copper. Copper is used, but so are a lot of other materials, such as gold, silver, rock crystal, bronze, lead and steel to name a few. In all cases the correct mixture of metal must be used depending on the type of Yantra that is to be created. This smelting of various types of materials can take a lot of time an effort, and is the main reason why it is a difficult to find genuine Yantra. There are Yantra in some homes in India, which were created many generations ago, and are provided a special place within the home. These are very likely to have been genuine Yantra created at a time when Yantra's were hand crafted by known and trusted Tantric's to bless and protect the home. This crafting tradition is unfortunately dying out and this has caused some problems with some Tantric practitioner's who used to rely on skilled metal craftsmen to provide some of materials needed to create Yantra. The craft of metal working has been in development almost uninterrupted in India for over five thousand years, and was the birth of many advanced metal working methods. Some

Yantra

of these methods were employed in weaponry for example to create strong, durable and effective fighting tools. There are some families who continue to pass on these traditional metal working methods, and there are also some Tantric's who are skilled in metal working to not require the need of another metal crafter to provide the materials for creation of Yantra. The following three images are: gold and copper plate (this page), smelted gold and silver (p.76), smelted copper and gold (p.76), and a completed final smelted peice before final beating and pressing (p.77).

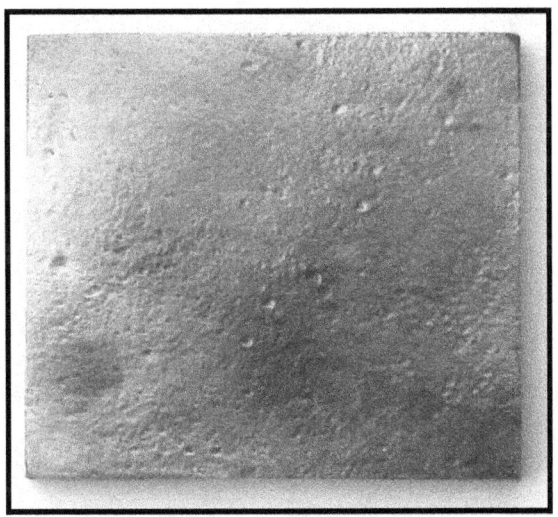

Yantra

Writing instrument for Yantra

The common writing instrument used is a quill made from a material as denoted by the Yantra to be created. This can be from jasmine or pomegranate wood, or made from various metals. Bird feathers, or branches of a particular tree can also be used. If ink is used, this is also created according to the type of Yantra to be made, and can be composed of turmeric or other colours ground from raw materials. For inscribing onto metal, the usual instrument will be a stronger pointed metal, or a specially created, pointed stone which is hard enough to inscribe with. Some Tantric's will keep their own special energised implement solely for the purpose of inscribing metals.

Time and place

Time (mahurat), and place, is denoted by the type of Yantra that needs to be created. In general those Yantra which are created for causing good are generally started early in the morning whilst those created to cause negative effects are started in the evening.

The hours of the day also play an important part and are related to the planets. Certain planets have been identified by Vedic astrologers to rule particular hours and this thus denotes the appropriate time for various rituals during the

Yantra

Yantra creation process. The table below lists the planets and types of Yantra which can be created.

HORA OF PLANET	PURPOSE
Jupiter	All Yantra's for good causes such as love, affection and the cure of diseases.
Venus & Mercury	For Yantra's related to love affairs, Mohan, Vashi Karan, Aakarshan, Business and Sale, and control of one's speech
Sun	For love, disease, affection, power authority, and successful meetings with superiors/dignitaries.
Saturn	To cause harm.
Mars	Litigation, overcoming enemies, and for creating differences between people.
Moon	Love, affection and attraction between the sexes.

Not only are specific hours important but so are the months, and these are linked with zodiac signs. Below is a table to illustrate this.

Note that the zodiacal signs are the Western equivalent of the original Vedic zodiac signs.

Zodiac Sign	Application
Aries	Yantra for monetary purposes
Taurus	Yantra's for harm
Gemini	Yantra for harm to others children
Cancer	Yantra for meditative yogic practices
Leo	Yantra for mental harm
Virgo	Yantra's for wealth and power
Libra	Any Yantra for beneficial purposes
Scorpio	Yantra for political and worldly power
Sagittarius	Yantra for esteem and self confidence
Capricorn	Any Yantra
Aquarius	Yantra for wealth and meditative practice
Pisces	Yantra for harm

Drawing of Yantra

The perfect geometrical shapes used when drawing some Yantra require a great deal of practice and instruction to get right. If we take for example a popular Sri Yantra shape, one can see the particular features which make up a Yantra, and one can understand why it can be extremely difficult to draw one.

As can be seen the nine triangles are interconnected to all of the other triangles within the Yantra, and these must touch at specified points to be considered a true Yantra. If even one triangle is incorrectly placed it will lose the interconnections between other points and therefore cause an imbalance in the Yantra. Another important aspect is the correct placement of the Bindu (dot), within the central plane of the Yantra. Again the incorrect position of the Bindu leads to an imbalance in the Yantra, and this will occur if the design of the Yantra is incorrect.

Triangles

What exactly is a triangle when we look at a Yantra? It begins first by defining the centre of a triangle which can represent different points. This is not the case for an equilateral triangle where all points coincide. So, for other types of triangle, one point can be the orthocenter, and which is the intersection of the lines from each vertex which meet the opposing sides perpendicularly, and are called the altitudes. Actually for any triangle, the altitudes always meet at the same point. The second is the circumcentre, which is the intersection of the perpendiculars when drawn from the halfway points of the sides. These lines always meet whichever triangle we are looking at. The third is the centroid, which is the intersection of the lines that go from the vertex to the midpoints of the opposing lines. Again, these always meet whatever triangle we are looking at. Finally we have the midcircle which every triangle will have, and is a circle that passes through the midpoints of each side, and also the intersection of the sides and the altitudes.

The Bindu

The bindu holds quite an important and significant place in the Yantra. The bindu is both a point of origin and the point of ending, and it is this duality which provides the Bindu such a significance. As the Upanishads say 'God being the unmovable mover, the One behind all events in the cosmos, is the still point around which everything revolves'. The point is therefore that from which everything is created, and into which everything dissolves.

Quantum world, sacred geometry and Yantra.

Embedded within all life is a form of geometry that is termed as sacred geometry. Sacred geometry is the representation of the energy vibrations in the world around us. The vibratory energy is conceptualized in Vedic texts as dual energies, in the form of Siva and Shakti. Similarly we have feminine and masculine energy channels within the body which features in Yogic and Tantric practice. Siva and Shakti are thus represented in Yantra by the triangles. These triangles represent various dimensional possibilities (and become a sacred geometric shape), and an instrument to harness and transform energies not only of the world around us, but of the person who is creating the Yantra. This is why the creation of the Yantra is not simply a matter of stamping out a copper sheet and inscribing mystical symbols or shapes upon it.

One must consider Yantra then, as not only a representation of sacred geometry, but also as a manipulator of energy (once charged), which has its influence on many levels of the physical and non-physical world.

Fibonacci sequence

The Fibonacci sequence in mathematics relates to a particular sequence of numbers and which has been used in the concept of the 'golden ratio' . What makes the sequence of numbers quite interesting is that they appear in biological arrangements, such as for example in the arrangement of a pine cone, or the sprouts of a pineapple. The sequence itself was discovered many years earlier by Indian scholars around 200bc and possibly earlier. This sequence is also harnessed within Yantra, and can be discerned by making calculations using the triangles. Furthermore ancient Hindu temples made use of higher mathematical concepts represented in the way that temples were designed and constructed. Some researchers have suggested that the designer's would have had to make complex calculations, such that it would take an extremely long time for modern computers to calculate. One very interesting aspect of the largest triangle within the Yantra is the angle of the base which is fifty degrees. This shares the same angle as the base of the Great Pyramid at

Gizeh, and using dimensions of the pyramid, one is able to derive the golden ratio, and be able to see links between pi and phi, and again this is reflected within the Yantra. This linkage with Hinduism and the Pyramids is quite interesting as a verse from the Gita was discovered inscribed on a pyramid excavated in 1967. The verse is a commonly known verse which translated says;

'As a person puts on a new garment, giving up the old ones, the soul similarly accepts a new material body giving up the old and useless ones'.

Pythagoras of Samos is known for his famous theorem on right angled triangles that bears his name, and has provided the basis for further mathematical applications which extend to higher dimensional spaces, and other types of triangles. Despite the theorem bearing Pythagoras's name there is evidence of knowledge and application of the theorem in ancient India (for example in the Baudhayana Sulba Sutra).

Indeed mathematics feature in many Vedic texts and a common idea is that the creation, standing and destruction of the universe happens in a very mathematical form. Mathematics was quite highly developed in ancient Vedic times, and some amazing feats of mathematical skills that were developed by Vedic mathematicians have over time been lost. What we have instead are stories of amazing mathematical feats. For example there is an ancient Vedic story of two kings walking in a forest. One of the kings said to the other that he could count all of the leaves on the tree just by looking at it, and on doing so provided the figure. The other king did not believe this and proceeded to pull off the leaves one by one counting them as he did so. When finished, the king was amazed to find that the other king had indeed provided the correct figure.

Use of Mantras

Tantra makes use of both Yantra and Mantra, and these are essentially inseparable from each other. The first part of the book explored how and where Mantra were derived from. It was also explained that Mantra's have been thus passed down from Saints and Yogis who having used them for thousands of years, were able to prove to themselves the effectiveness of them for use in Tantric work.

The word Mantra itself is a Sanskrit word. Man is derived from manana, which means to think deeply, and 'tra' is from Trana, to mean deliverance. A Mantra is made up of certain attributes which include the metre, the seed sounds, the energy sounds, and the supports which then completes the structure of the Mantra. The chanting of Mantra's create not only a physical sound but also a vibration within the energy field, and in the Veda's it is said that the entire cosmic creation began with a sound. These patterns of energies created using sound are able to affect the subtle and material world, and are able to pierce through all levels of existence. Linking in with the concept of Chakra's, certain sounds are able to affect the chakra's directly.

The use of Mantra is difficult in that Mantras have to be spoken the right way (almost as if it is a musical tone), using the right patterns and tone of voice. Such is the importance of this that a Guru is often sought to properly guide and instruct in the proper pattern and specific tone for particular Mantra. Any deviations from the proper sounds of the Mantra can lead to a loss of power, and the benefits derived from them are dissipated. Scientific studies into sound have in recent years provided evidence in the way sound waves interact with the environment. In particular, the visual representation of sounds has revealed remarkable similarity to Yantra designs. The term used for this particular type of study is Cymatics and various instruments are employed in order to visually display the sound patterns of particular sounds. The growth of interest in this area of study has also led to amateur scientists discovering further and innovative ways of capturing sounds physically. The origin of Cymatics is related to Hans Jenny who in 1967, published the first volume of his book called 'Cymatics: The Study of Wave Phenomena', with a second volume which came out in 1972. Hans Jenny was a scientist who was able to produce photographs of the effects of sound using various materials (liquids, powders and pastes). He also made use of a tonoscope, which was in effect a way to transmit sound to allow the correct representation of it on a plate of quartz sand. It has been found that when the sacred sound of 'aum' is spoken in the correct tone, the pattern which is generated is that of a Yantra (a sri Yantra).

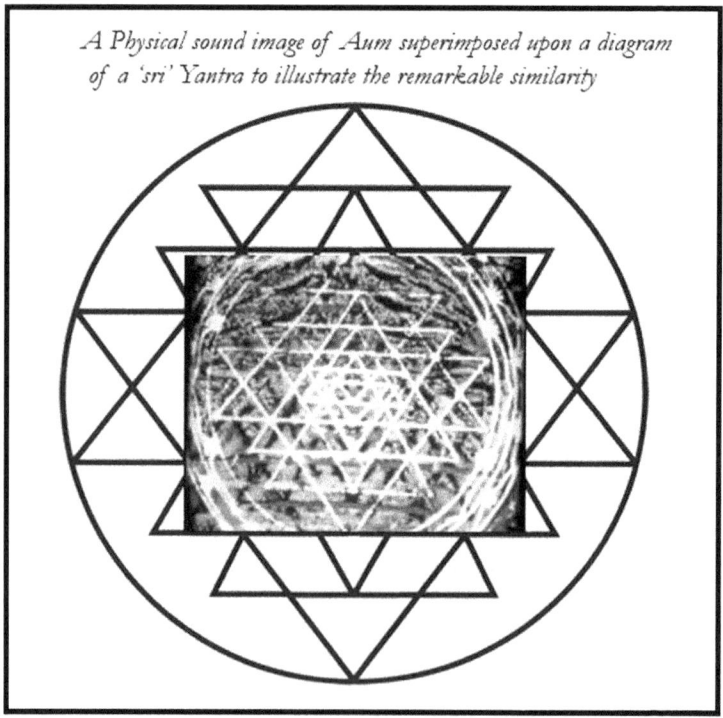

A Physical sound image of Aum superimposed upon a diagram of a 'sri' Yantra to illustrate the remarkable similarity

Mantra's thus are considered capable of causing effects on so many levels and are able to give a transformational effect on the person chanting the Mantra. There is also some work conducted by Mrs. Watts Hughes who wrote 'Voice

Figures'. Using an instrument called an Eidophone which consisted of a tube, receiver and a membrane upon which various materials such as powders or seeds were placed. She was able to demonstrate various forms and geological figures which appeared when songs or sounds were introduced to the Eidophone. For example a Bengali hymn was sung by a student and the figure of Bhairava appeared complete with his vehicle (dog). This hymn was a hymn to Bhairava and thus illustrates again how the Mantra and prayers have an effect on the physical world.

Most if not all Mantra will use the syllable of Aum. This is considered as the most sacred syllable of all because it is said to be the first sound of the Universe, from which every other sound emerged. It is the very basis of every other sacred Mantra or prayers.

There are some common Mantras used throughout Hindu homes which actually form part of the prayers during ceremony's, because Mantra's originate from the Veda's. However, these Mantra's are also used on an individual basis and chanted to bring about positive effects which have been reported over thousands of years, and explains why they are in popular common usage. These particular types of Mantra are mostly what are called 'seed' Mantra. A list is provided of these well-known prayer/Mantra with details of their particular benefits.

Gayatri Mantra

This Mantra is based on a verse in the Rigveda and is as follows:

Om bhur burva swaha
Tat savitur vareneyam
Bhargo devasya dhimahi
Dhiyo yon na prachordoya

The Gayatri mantra is made up of the energies of 24 single energies. It is for this reason that the Gayatri mantra is so revered and so widely known and prescribed. The following describes each of the twenty four energies which when combined into the mantra above, provides the combined benefits of these energies.

1: Ganesh Gayatri-removal of all obstacles.
2: Vishnu Gayatri-for the protection of the family
3: Shiva Gayatri-removal of problems and to bring peace and prosperity
4: Brahma Gayatri-to enhance productivity
5: Ram Gayatri-to enhance ones status in the world
6: Krishna Gayatri-for success in employment
7: Indra Gyatri-for protection in war and aggression
8: Hanuman Gayatri-for selfless service
9: Surya Gayatri-for relief from health problems
10: Chandra Gayatri-to calm nerves from all worries

11: Yama Gayatri-to calm fear of death
12: Varuna Gayatri-to increase love between male and female
13: Narayan Gayatri-to increase power in all administrative tasks
14: Narsingh Gayatri-for assistance with helping others
15: Durga Gayatri-for overcoming obstacles and enemies
16:Lakshmi Gayatri-for wealth and success
17: Radha Gayatri-to increase love of the divine
18: Sita Gayatri-to assist with work on oneself
19: Sarawati Gayatri-for knowledge, wisdom and learning
20: Agni Gayatri-to provide power to all organs, the mind and the spiritual body
21: Prithvi Gayatri-for co-operation and patience
22: Kam Gayatri-for sexual power and all related functions
23: Hans Gayatri-to increase the powers of analysis
24: Hayagri Gayatri-to increase courage and diminish fears

Hare Krishna Mantra

Although now strongly associated with the Hare Krishna movement, this Mantra has long been part of Hindu culture. The Mantra is thus;

Hare Krishna Hare Krishna
Krishna Krishna Hare Hare
Hare Rama Hare Rama
Ram Ram Hare Hare

This Mantra is referred by many scholars as a maha-Mantra

or great Mantra, because it is said that the chanting of this Mantra is the easiest way of meditation and purification and eventually leads to a transformation of self.

Tantric Mantra

Apart from the commonly used Mantra described in the preceding pages, there are Mantra specifically within Tantric practice. When used within Tantric practice it can be either alongside the creation or charging of a Yantra, or used entirely on its own. When used on their own they are employed within a particular ritual, and just as there are categories of use for Yantra there are categories for use of Mantra. So for example Mantra to cause harm or bringing back someone who has been lost.

Much of Tantric Mantra's are secret such is their power, and are only passed on from one to another within a guru/ disciple relationship. Sometimes Mantra are created anew for a particular person to recite to bring about effects, and these mantra will have in turn revealed to the Guru through meditation. A Mantra can be made live in five ways. The first can be from writing the mantra down and reciting it in this way. The second through the common form of speaking, the third through a whisper, fourth via meditation upon a mantra, and the last through constant unbroken internal repetition (sometimes termed as japa).

Yantra, Mantra and Hemispheric Synchronisation

Since the 1960's there has been a lot of research conducted on the brain and its chemical and physiological workings. One of the most interesting developments has been in the understanding of brainwaves, and the differences in the frequencies when sleeping to when wide awake. For example in deep sleep the dominant frequency is around the delta range (0.4 to 4Hz), whilst Yogi's in meditation will flutter around the theta frequency of 4-8Hz. Further research and experimentation has found that these frequencies could be induced by the application of flashing lights that correspond to the frequency required. This effect was likened to a person sitting watching a fire, where the flames flicker to a certain frequency and which, after some time, cause the person to enter a light meditative state. Other research revealed that when two separate frequencies of sounds were played via headphones, the brain would begin to exhibit a frequency follow response in the brain. In detecting the phase variance, the brain would begin to create a third signal (a binaural beat), equal to the difference between the two frequencies. In other words, if one ear was fed a signal of 100hz, and the other 105hz, a third signal would be created by the brain of 5hz, and become the dominant frequency. This experimentation into binaural beats led to an explosion of work by psychologists and sound technologists to explore ways of driving the brain to various states. Further work mapping brain states whilst driving the brain, revealed that not only was the brain able to follow the frequencies, it also exhibited brainwave synchronisation. In other words, both hemispheres of the brain exhibited the dominant frequency. Why this is unusual is that in the majority of people the frequencies are not coherent for both sides of the brain. There is a dominance of one side of the brain depending on the person and the task at hand. When both sides of the brain are working coherently there is a harmony which yields itself to better performance at whatever task is being conducted. The brain thus is able to function better as both sides of the brain are working towards the same ends. There is a great deal of published academic research that can be explored further upon this topic if one wishes to. The point to raise is that the use of Mantra, and Yantra also make use of the idea of brain synchronisation. The following chart illustrates the differences between a Yantra and Mantra, and the second chart illustrates the two sides of the brain and what they are responsible for.

Yantra

Mantra	Yantra
Words	Form
Sounds	Colour
Logic	Creativity
Letters	
Lists	
Organisation	
Timing	
Repetition	

Left Brain
Verbal, focusing on words, symbols, numbers
Analytical, led by logic
Process ideas sequentially, step by step
Words used to remember things, remember names
Make logical deductions from information
Good at keeping track of time
Listen to what is being said-detail of the words
Right Brain
Visual, focusing on images, patterns
Intuitive, led by feelings
See the whole first, then the details
Listen to how something is being said-rhythm, space between words

As can be seen there is a remarkable similarity between the left and right brain and Mantra and Yantra. We thus see the synergistic way in which Yantra and Mantra work together, and it follows that hemispheric synchronisation does take place within the Tantric practitioner (and provides a suitable vehicle for promoting meditative states).

Part 3: Tantrism and Yantra in Practice

Introduction

This chapter contains descriptions of real Tantric practices and illustrates further the part Yantra and Mantra play in them. Some detail has been deliberately omitted as requested by those who have shared the information to the researchers. This is so as to prevent anyone from carrying out these practices without the correct instruction or guidance. The images reffered to are in Part 5 of the book (page 141).

One could categorise Tantric practices in two ways. The first can be those practices which are for personal benefit and enhancement of the Tantric. For example, the development and enhancement of particular powers to assist towards the ultimate goal of liberation. The other category can be those practices which are carried out for and on behalf of other people, such as for example to help with relationship troubles or gain material wealth. It is this second category of practices which are described in this part the book.

Only a few examples are provided here, however there can be many different practices, rituals, or variations of these to achieve the same aims. In the real world, the Tantric will choose a particular ritual or practice based upon his or own abilities, experience and particular tradition. Some traditions will favour the use of certain materials whilst others will lean heavily on the use of Mantra. Some purposes can and will only be done by a particular Tantric practitioner, such as for example those that are to cause harm to someone. The Tantric's who are able to do this are very difficult to find because they prefer seclusion as most of their general practices, and ways of living will defy social norms. They can often be found at cremation grounds and will make use of some materials there as part of their Tantric practice and rituals (soil/ash from a recently buried or cremated person, human bones and so forth).

Specific Uses for Yantra

General astrological Yantra

It is common practice in India that a birth chart is created as soon as the child is born. This is created by an astrologer and within this chart certain negative influences of planets are described. Yantra are then prescribed in order to reduce the effects of these negative planets and to enhance any neutral and beneficial planets. The creation of this Yantra is largely conducted by the astrologers themselves, however these are in turn purchased off the shelf or inscribed on to a blank copper plate, or on paper by the astrologer. This therefore ends up as a nonworking Yantra as it involves none of the Vedic processes that are needed to create a real Yantra and the family do not see any benefits for their child.

Yantra

Astrological Yantra are related to particular planets (including the Sun) and the correct one is determined by the childs astrological chart as shown.

Yantra

Planet	Application
Sun	If the Sun is situated in a negative house it can cause some diseases.
Moon	The moon if in a negative house causes problems with any water related health issues. This includes menstruation and urinary systems.
Mars	The negative influence of Mars leads to marital problems. Blood related problems are also associated with this planet as are accidents.
Mercury	Negative aspects include loss through fire or via weather systems such as storms and lightning.
Jupiter	Negative influences here will affect loss of status and power.
Venus	Venus is linked to sexual organs and here problems can occur.
Saturn	Negative effects include loss of business or work
Uranus	Negative aspects relate to skin conditions. This includes for example acne, scarring, spots and so forth.
Neptune	Neptune if situated in a negative aspect will cause problems with status and to immoral activity.
Pluto	Pluto has similar to mars effect although slightly less power full

Enhance power and authority leading to financial success.

One of the Yantra's created for this purpose is the Sri Yantra (image 4), and was a very popular one used during ancient times for kings and those in political office. Such is its popularity that it continues to be created for political leaders in India. The particular Mantra that is used during the creation of this Yantra is as follows;

'Om Shareen, Hareeng, Kaleeng, Hareeng, Sri Mahalakhsmaiya Namah'

The material used for this Yantra will be based on the persons astrological chart as will any particular rituals during its creation (in general Gold, silver or copper will be the main constituents). The Yantra is worn anywhere on the body as long as it makes contact with the skin.

Education/Knowledge

BagalaMukhi Yantra
This Yantra (image 3), is created in relationship to the person's astrological chart, and created during a particular moon position. This Yantra, as part of the ritual requires daily recitation of a Mantra by the Tantric for 45 days, and is required to wear yellow in clothing as well utilise yellow colour materials. The Tantric practitioner requires complete

Yantra

abstinence from sex and any consumption of animal foods (including eggs). Once the Yantra is created it must be worn anywhere close to the body, and the person is required to avoid meat products and sexual intercourse on Tuesdays. The Yantra can be fitted into a ring depending on the skill of the creator. But in general the Yantra is too large for this and so alternatively it is enclosed within a locket and worn around the neck or around the right arm.

Saraswati Yantra

This is a useful Yantra (image 1), when a person is not gifted with a good intellect due to lack of access to education. It helps to sharpen the mind and to better understand difficult concepts, and provides assistance in studies and examinations.

Lalita Thrisathi

This Yantra (image 21), assists with gaining knowledge over the self. It is primarily used for those undergoing spiritual work on themselves. In general it is created for those of older age who have retired from work, and other responsibilities, and now wish to focus on their own self and spiritual development. This Yantra is created using Copper, although it can also be inscribed onto a particular leaf using vermillion paste. The only difference is that the leaf has a short longevity and so requires it to be remade once the Yantra starts to fade. The idea with using the leaf is that the person is taught how to draw the Yantra, and how to speak the correct Mantra during its creation. The person then takes over creating their own Yantra, and in turn it helps with their spiritual work.

Guru Yantra

For those wanting spiritual knowledge, the Yantra in image 33 is created. It is created by a guru once he has agreed to pass on the knowledge to the initiate.

Deepa Yantra

This Yantra (image 16, 8), assists with all memory issues. It helps retention and recall of facts, figures, and processes and so is quite popular for all those undergoing study which culminates in exams. The Yantra can only be created on the night of Divali. A blank copper plate is prepared before hand (prior to Divali night) by smelting and flattening copper to a thin square size. The Yantra is then placed on an altar on which a bed of rice is built and where the Yantra is placed. The rituals take place during Divali night, and the Yantra is completed by the time the first rays of the sun are seen. The Yantra must be worn before noon that same day.

Relationships/married life

Saraswati Yantra

This Yantra (image 9), is created for both partners if there are difficulties. It can also be created for one person to assist in relationships or help with finding a life partner.

Subhagya Vijay Yantra

This Yantra (image 2) is used for people to be able to attract members of the opposite sex. The Yantra is carved out on a metal plate made up of the correct mix of copper, gold and silver. The main difficulty in creating this Yantra is the need to make it small enough to be able to be worn around the arm for men (around the neck for women). The problem that occurs is that the mixture of metals if not correctly smelted together will lead to a large piece of metal that is of an incorrect size for the Yantra. This piece then either has to be used (with the discomfort of wearing a large piece), or the Yantra discarded. The metal can not be simply melted down again to be re-used as the correct composition of each of the metals will no longer be the same as when started.

Another variation of this type of Yantra, is when an attraction between two identified individuals is required. The Yantra shown in image 11, and is written on copper plate (and one other metal decided by the two people's astrological chart). This plate is worn by one of the people. The other requires a Yantra written on a flattened edible material which is then dissolved in water and drunk by the other person.

Here is an example of the experience of using such a Yantra recorded by one of the researchers. The background to this was that a couple was arranged to be married by the families. In this case neither of the two had met before the marriage, and after the marriage it was apparent that there were difficulties between them. The girl spoke of the problems to her mother who then met with the mother of the boy and together it was decided that advice from a Guru be sought, who suggested a Yantra. The following is the translated word from the girl;

'I was given a copper plate Yantra to wear around my neck and I was given a piece of Ghor (jaggery) that had been mixed with Ghee and flattened into a small square. I was given the instruction to recite a Mantra before incorporating this square ghor yantra into a meal prepared for my husband (without his knowledge). I prepared a sweet milk dessert which I gave my husband to drink. The effects happened gradually over the week. My husband started to converse with me, and I with him and he started to be a lot more humorous with me. I also noticed a change within me. There had been a long-term feeling of worry within me, which only after wearing the Yantra did I notice and paid attention to it. By my focus upon it, it began to no longer have power over me and in three weeks it was replaced by a certain joyness. I and my husband had not had any bed relations since marriage, but within a month me and my husband were having normal relations and this in turn brought us closer together not only in mind but in body too'.

Lalita Yantra

This Yantra is mainly for those wishing to attract people and can be used for women or men. Copper is used in the construction of the Yantra and initially inscribed using a paste composed of honey and crushed honeycomb. Charging takes 8 days facing north and recitations of a Mantra two thousand times each day:

'Om Shri Dev Duttam Me Vashmanye Swaha'.

Vashikaran Yantra

This Yantra (image 26), is for married women whose husbands are involved with other females. This is an effective Yantra to quash the husbands attraction to the other female. The Yantra is created on a Monday using gold and copper. The charging takes place over 7 days. On the eight day the woman must take part in a simple blessing ceremony where she is presented with her Yantra. The Yantra is taken home and placed under the couples bed. If the husband is not sleeping in the same bed as his wife then the Yantra must be placed under his bed. This Yantra therefore will only work for those husbands who are still living with their wife, and will not work if the husband has already left the marital home and has his bed elsewhere.

Peace Yantra

This is a large Yantra to be kept in the home (image 24). A small amount of Gold is mixed with silver and is created over a period of one month. Due to the large size of this Yantra, the amount of gold used can be considerable and therefore very costly. The Yantra bring peace to the home, and keeps in check arguments and disagreements.

Wealth and material comforts

Kaliyan Yantra

A Kaliyan Yantra (image 36), is created according to a person's astrological chart. In particular this is used when Saturn plays a non-beneficial part in a person's astrological chart and will help to limit the harmful effects on the person's life. This particular Yantra requires a great many rituals to create and usually involves more than one Tantric when carrying them out.

Sri Bhairon Yantra

This Yantra (image 29), involves one thousand recitations over 41 days and takes place during the night. Alcohol is offered to a deity among other items depending on the particular day of the week. It is composed of silver and gold, but can also be created from Rock crystal (which is very rare).

Dhumavati Yantra

Copper, and silver is used for this Yantra mixed to a portion of 60:40. This Yantra (image 28), completes its creation during the night at a cremation ground. The Tantric practitioner must remain unclothed throughout the procedure. During the night various rituals take place, along with recitations of particular Mantra's which concludes when the first rays of the sun are seen.

Gauri Shankar Yantra

Copper and steel is needed for this Yantra (image 20), smelted to the proportion of 70:30. It must be created on a Monday or Thursday.

Fame and fortune

This Yantra assists anyone to gain fame and therefore fortune in their particular craft. Two Yantra are created (image 27), and one is kept in the home whilst the other is worn. A running river is required, as the Yantra must be dipped numerous times in the river whilst mantra are spoken.

Dipa Yantra

This Yantra (image 31), can only be created during the months of Holi, Divali or Shivatri. Gold and copper is mixed together in equal portions. After charging (over 20 days), the Yantra is then placed within the home, or home temple. The following Mantra is recited at least once every year to ensure charging is maintained.

Business success

Foundation Yantra

A Yantra can be created to be placed within the foundations of a new business location (image 19). This is a lengthy and costly process as it requires large amounts of various metals. It is therefore only used by those who can afford to do so. In ancient times such Yantra were placed at places of commerce and the costs were bourne by the King of that region.

Wall Yantra

The Yantra shown in image 27, is used to increase sales and is created using pure gold (plus one more element determined by the particular location of the business). The Yantra after appropriate rituals is fixed within the place of business and certain Mantra recited over 45 days. In some cases an additional Yantra is affixed above the main entrance doorway.

Success in trades

This Yantra (image 28), was commonly created for craftsman and artisans such as those involved with woodworking, construction, clothes making, and sculpture's. It is equally applicable for modern craft workers and those in specialised trades. The Yantra is smelted using gold and silver, along with some part of the tool of the trade. For example a carpenter would provide some slivers of his mallet, which would be smelted with the metals (and burnt off). Two Yantra are created, one of which is to be worn, and the other to be kept along with the instruments of the trade.

Promotion

This Yantra assists with gaining promotion in whatever work one undertakes. In ancient times it was in use for young apprentices who wished to be promoted to higher positions. Yantra in image 35 is created using a mix of gold and copper. The Yantra must be worn during the day, and at night it is to be kept among the tools of the trade, such as a toolbox, paper pad, or on a computer.

Protection

Mrit Sanjivani Yantra

Copper and silver is melted together in a 80:20 combination. The blank plate must be left beside a banyan tree for 45 days. The plate is then carved out with a Yantra and Mantra recited over 45 days along with various offerings (fruits, rice, milk, sugar, mustard etc), and can involve ten thousand Mantras. The Yantra (image 22), is worn by the person and offers protection from diseases with other general beneficial effects.

Mangal Yantra

This Yantra (image 10), is created using pure gold. The house where the Yantra is due to placed in, is where a puja (worship) is performed. This allows the house and its occupants to receive the benefits of the Yantra. It offers occupants protection from accidents, cuts and wounds, as well as recovery from operations. This Yantra is very powerful and allows the occupants of the house to perform additional worship upon it to gain specific benefits. For example to heal separations between two people, calm bad tempers, or to help unmarried girls to find partners. In some cases this same Yantra can be worn for a limited period of time to help with specific problems. For example to help someone who is shy and unable to say what is on their minds, can wear such a Yantra at a meeting where he is required to speak.

Release from enclosures

This Yantra can be used whenever the person is in a situation where they are trapped. This can mean physical entrapment such as a prison, or it can mean being trapped by debts. The

Yantra

Yantra in image 17 is created over two weeks, and made using copper plates. Up to eight of these Yantra are created, one to be kept on the person, and the others to be distributed among all rooms of the house. Daily worship of all Yantra is required.

Protection from enemies

For those with constant problems with others arising through jealously or envy, the Yantra in images 32 or 40 are created on a full moon. The Yantra is completed in one night and is a mix of silver and copper. The Yantra is to be worn around the neck at all times.

Karia Yantra

This Yantra (image 30), is a very common one seen at market stalls and online stores. It is also common to see this Yantra hung in many Hindu homes. This is because it is a good all round Yantra and the genuine ones have proven their effectiveness for many people.

Gold, copper and silver along with some other elements are melted together and rolled into thin sheets. The sheets are then folded four times and melted again and beaten until it becomes a solid flat plate. A circle is carved which is divided into seven equal windows, and in each window a symbol and number is inscribed. The numbers have a special significance as well as the symbols which are described on the next page.

Yantra

The Yantra is hung inside the entrance to the house or alternatively kept inside a temple.

Snake	Helps with knowledge, and healing
Stringed Instrument	Helps with confidence and creates happiness
Tree	Helps the family move forward positively and plans come to fruition
Jewels	Denotes prosperity
Sun	Helps individuals to be courageous and bestows good fortune on those whom people depend on
Arrow	Protects against evil eye and from those who try to throw 'arrows' at the family in order to create problems
Ship	Ensure smooth sailing no matter if the waters are rough and choppy.

Health Yantra

<u>Durga Shashuma</u>

This Yantra is especially for those suffering from any watery ailments. This includes menstruation problems and urinary disorders. It is generally created for younger women at an early developmental stage to ensure breasts and menstruation development occur in a healthy manner. This Yantra requires a pure gold plate, and the charging process lasts six days facing eastward. Once created the Yantra (image 15), can be worn around the arm or neck.

Garbh Stampan

Pure gold, copper and silver is used for this yantra (image 25), and it is mainly used for male fertility problems, but it can be useful for male urinary problems. A thousand recitations of Mantra have to be completed over six days. On the seventh day the creator of the Yantra must dip the Yantra in female vaginal pre-orgasmic secretions. These secretions must have been collected the day before as part of Tantric energy rituals.

Headaches & tension

This Yantra (image 18), is to be worn at night when sleeping. It must be kept on the forehead and attached using orange cloth. This assists with tension headaches, migraine, and also calms the mind from worries. In ancient times it was used as a method to reduce internal brain swellings.

Bhok Kes Yantra

This Yantra (image 7), assists with the proper functioning of bodily processes. In particular for females it helps those of younger age and assists with the proper development of the body.

To cause death

A Sri Bhairon Yantra is created, but in this case the Tantric practitioner must sit at a crossroad at midnight and recite a Mantra ten thousand times.

The Yantra (image 12), is kept with the Tantric until the death has occurred which takes a month. After this the Yantra must then be destroyed by Mantra and then immersed in to the Ganges.

To cause difficulties between people

A Yantra (image 40), is created with the use of the blood of an owl, crow and the menstruation of a widowed woman. This blood is mixed together to create an ink, whilst a pen is made from a crow's wing. A Yantra is written on paper and Mantra recitations are made which include the name of the people that the Yantra requires to effect. The Yantra is then placed in the house of the person, or persons. From then on, it will cause arguments from even the smallest things.

Another type of Yantra can also be made using materials obtained from the two individuals. During certain rituals and Mantra, these materials are thrown in to a fire which causes the breakup of the two people. This is effective for occasions where it may not be possible to visit the home of the person to place a Yantra.

Finding about missing person/bringing a missing person back

One ancient method was to write a Yantra (image 36), in black ink on mango leaf and placed in a bucket which was then lowered down into a well. Certain sounds would then emanate from the well which would provide clues about the missing person. A total absence of sound would mean the person was alive, but mystery still surrounded the whereabouts. In order to bring a missing person back, a Yantra would be written and mounted on a spinning wheel. A girl who had reached puberty (but a virgin) would be required to spin the wheel seven times after which she would be required to place the wheel into the ground near the house of the missing person.

Childbirth

For those who desire birth of a son, the Yantra in image 38 is created by drawing in orange ink onto a large leaf. The leaf is folded and is to be kept in a clay pot in full sun for one month. Each day of that month, the Gayatri mantra must be recited as soon as the first rays of the sun reach the clay pot in the morning. The Yantra in image 7 is also used but this can also be utilised for assisting with problems from enemies.

Astrological problems

Some planets have a negative effect on individuals and there are what are termed as Planetary Yantra's which are used to help in these cases. The creation of such Yantra must occur at the correct time (bright phase of the planet) and if possible, the person for whom the Yantra is to be made must also be present. If this is not possible then an article belonging to the person can be used (fingernail, lock of hair). The type of metal used for the Yantra is determined by the planet, and once the ritual/Mantra is complete, the Yantra (image 37), is placed within another metal enclosure which is then worn by the individual.

Yantra

PART 4
Obtaining a Yantra

Introduction

Unfortunately the whole subject of obtaining Yantra has caused a great deal of confusion and misinformation. Visit any market in India and one can see a vast array of Yantra being offered for sale. It may be the case that these general Yantra are energised to some degree however such energies cannot be held in these Yantra for a great deal of time and so after a year it has ceased to be of any practical use. So of the small percentage that are energised in such a way (and attract a slightly larger cost premium), the others offered on markets provide nothing but visual appeal when hung on walls, or kept in home temples.

With the growth of online marketplaces, the selling of such Yantra has also multiplied and has led to an even bigger growth of non-genuine Yantra. Production of such mass market Yantra has been traced back to China where raw materials are cheap, as are production costs. In fact latest statistics show that fifty-five percent of Yantra's being sold in India were imported from China. This has led to many people unknowingly purchasing Yantra that have no real power, and one can understand how such people can lose faith in Yantra which do not appear to be changing anything within their life situation.

This part of the book provides some guidance on obtaining

Yantra for personal use. The first thing one requires is a maker of Yantra and as was described in preceding parts, finding a maker of genuine Yantra can be a very difficult task. A novice visitor to India on asking around for someone to make a genuine Yantra maker, can be easily exploited and duped. This is in fact what happened to a couple of researchers and their experiences are described here and will assist in recognising signs to look out for. The following researchers were all Indian born and one may assume less likely to be taken advantage of, yet this was not the case.

Jamila Mistry

'I like the others was asked to blend in which was quite easy to do. I began by visiting a shop that sold a lot of Hindu religious items such as divos (lamps), incense and idols. I enquired with the seller if he knew where to get a genuine Yantra. At first he tried to say that his own Yantra were genuine, but I then told him I knew about Yantra and walked away. He called me back and then asked for me to come back later in the evening and he would be able to help. When I returned in the evening he had closed his shop and was waiting for me. He told me he could get a genuine Yantra made, but it would require two days and I would need to pay up-front. I then asked what details he required of me and he simply asked me my name and nothing else. I asked how a genuine Yantra could be made if he had not asked me my astrological data. His reply was that 'they know everything' to which I realised his product would not be a genuine Yantra , including the fact that I was dubious of his claim that the Yantra could be made in two days'.

<u>Rameshri Bhoguna</u>

'I had family in India and asked them to ask around for any contacts for genuine Yantra. I was given twelve names which were eventually narrowed down to three by process of elimination. This elimination process involved me visiting the people and asking some simple questions and if the answers were not satisfactory I did not proceed further. I then -revisited the three names left who seemed promising. The first one required the equivalent of five thousand dollars to proceed, with half to be paid up front. The second took me to a meeting of three other men who all appeared to be knowledgeable. However some of the answers to my questions were very dubious. For example I mentioned a health problem as well as a general problem with money to which I was told they could give me a super Yantra which would work for anything. However this required me to offer a yearly gift of gold to the amount of 5 ounces to a priest (this in addition to the Yantra fee of 1000 dollars equivalent). The third person told me a Yantra could be provided but required a pilgrimage which he would arrange and I would need to pay the costs. When I said I was not interested, he suggested a secret Mantra that would help instead. In all the process took 6 months to investigate and was unsuccessful'.

Over a few months, time and money was expended by researchers in order to track down families as well as individuals who were able to either create, or who knew someone who would be able to create, genuine Yantra. Those who were from a family tradition of Tantrism were discovered through various contacts and only possible when enough trust had built up between the researcher and the contact. This therefore is a difficult method of obtaining a Yantra, as the time taken to find the correct contact can be considerable. Furthermore extra verification processes then need to take place to ensure it is not part of a scam to dupe the enquirer and to make money.

The other method was to locate those who have taken the Tantric path and moved away from general society. These are often just called yogi's, priests, guru's, or holy men. One has to locate such a yogi who undertakes particular rituals and practices, and who is able to create Yantra. Many that were discovered did not offer to create Yantra for others, and any they did make were used for themselves for their own spiritual work. Some however could be persuaded to create Yantra, whilst others freely offered such services to all those who came to them. After the section below regarding purchasing from the internet, there is a guide to locating places in India which can assist anyone in procuring genuine Yantra.

Purchasing from the internet

The growth of internet shopping has offered another avenue for learning about, and purchasing Yantra.

Over a sixty websites were checked by researchers by ordering Yantra and then asking follow-up questions about the Yantra including things such as manufacturing methods, how they work, care of Yantra, packing, transportation and charging of Yantra. Of the hundred, only four were rated highly, and thus could be trusted to provide genuine Yantra. These are listed in the appendix on page 195.

All other websites although claiming to offer genuine Yantra, either did not collect the purchasers astrological data, (so could not possibly be creating personalised yantra), or even when such data was collected, they were not able to provide verifiable details on who exactly created the Yantra. If the creators of the Yantra could not be checked, then one can not be certain that the Yantra had been created according to traditional methods. Some websites were not able to provide answers to most basic Yantra questions, and in most cases it was clear that the questions were being fielded by sales-people employed in that regard, and therefore interested only in sales generation.

India: Obtaining Yantra

India is the best place (many argue the only) place to go to obtain a genuine Yantra. The general locations are described below. The maps that are referred to can be found in the next section and have been reproduced from researchers maps.

The locations were selected on the basis of how easy it was for the researchers to access the locations, and time taken to identify those who were able to create genuine Yantra.

The locations are listed below with some photo's for assistance. It may be the case that any landscape development work carried out since the map was made will make it difficult to find these. In such cases local knowledge will prove invaluable.

General advice

It is always important to check all relevant travel advice as provided from your home country. One of the best sources of travel advice is the website of the British Foreign and Commonwealth office. You should also make yourself fully aware of the particulars of India, and there are many good travel guides available which will provide important information about things such as money, facilities, accommodation and more.

The following location advice will assume that you have reached India and have found suitable accommodation, and are able to make travel arrangements to move to various locations in India.

Location: Nashik
Map 1
This resides near caves South West of Nashik, in an area called the Pandau Caves (photo P.132). Here there are around 20 yogi's who follow a branch of Tantrism and live around the caves and are known locally as the Grahaputra-Yamuanata's. The yogis were quite approachable and welcoming and happy to assist with any questions. They welcomed donations of foodstuffs and or plates/metal cups. These Yogis enter periods of meditation within and around the caves, and these occur during certain times of the year and can be from a week to a couple of months long. At such times therefore, they can not be approached.

Location: South India: Mahendrapalli
Map 2
Along the part of the river there are a series of stonewall dwellings as shown on the map. There are two families here whose Yantra work dates back many hundreds of years. The researchers were able to verify this from family records and being shown various artefacts. At the time of the research there was a few elders left who were still creating Yantra and stated that only one or two had taken on instruction and learning in order to carry on with this tradition. Whether this families long history of Yantra making die out in fifty years time uncertain.

Location Near Haridwar

Map 3

Haridwar is a popular pilgrimage place for Hindus and you will find a great deal of items for sale within the local market places. Some of the researchers were given some helpful advice on where particular Tantric followers could be located and these locations were sought out and found. A hill must be climbed which is called Kaliory. Chutmalpur is the closest village to the location required. It can be reached by Rickshaw which will drop you close to where the hill begins. Ensure you provide the village name as well as the name of the hill. This will ensure that even if the driver does not know the hill he will be able to take you to the village and obtain the location of the Hill.

Once you are at the Hill, there will be a well worn path that winds around the hill to the top. Ensure you are able to begin your climb early in the day and take enough water and other supplies.

You will reach an end to a path and will be greeted with a flattened area after which there will be a few large grey rocks with various markings. It will appear there is no way forward, however if you proceed to the right side of the rock and carefully walk along the side there is a cutout which will allow you entry into the cave (see image on page 133). There are steps down and you will see a lingham within the central plane of the cave room. There will be a priest there who told us he resides there permanently and is provided for by those who come to pray there. You will need to ask the priest about Yantra and whether there are any people there that can make them. The hill is very popular by Tantric followers and it would be rare to not find someone there who could make a Yantra. It will be the case however that you will have to provide your details and then return in a week or so to collect the Yantra. This is because the hill is a place where people travel to and Yantra's are always made at a particular place and where materials are on hand to make them.

Location: Near Hyderabad
Map 4
Near to Hyderabad is a place called Siddipet. The actual location is south from Siddipet.

Location: Khakati Near Sambhar Lake in Jaipur
Close to Jaipur and Sambhar Lake is a place called Khakati. You must travel further west of this location towards the lake where you will come across a lot of Yogis who live around the hills near the lake. There are a mix of Yogis here following varied traditional paths and you will need to make your own enquiries with them to ascertain who would be able to create Yantra for you.

Although the location provided is the main location and the easiest to get to. You can also travel around the very large lake and find yogi's along your travels. It is a pleasant location and you will find some hotels dotted not too far from the lake.

Location: Chattrapur South India: Ganjam
Located North east of Chattrapur is a small settlement of Ganjam. There are several families here that have long been involved in Tantric traditions and still to this day engage in

Yantra

various works for the public that visit there. Most of their work comes from the South and you will find a few market stalls setup there offering various Tantric tools. There are also some very good worksmiths here that also come from long family traditions in woodworking, metalworking, and gemstone work. A lot of good quality gemstones are worked here and it is a good place to pick up such souvenirs.

Bandaruvanipeta Village South India

Plenty of market stalls will be found here selling Yantra and other religious items. The researchers found very helpful sellers here who were able to provide addresses of people who lived in the village who created mass-market yantra for them. These people were however skilled and trained in creating personalised Yantra and there were at least five families living within this location who were verified by the researchers. You can also find Yogis further towards the coast as well as south towards the Hanuman Temple.

Yantra

Location Maps

Map 1

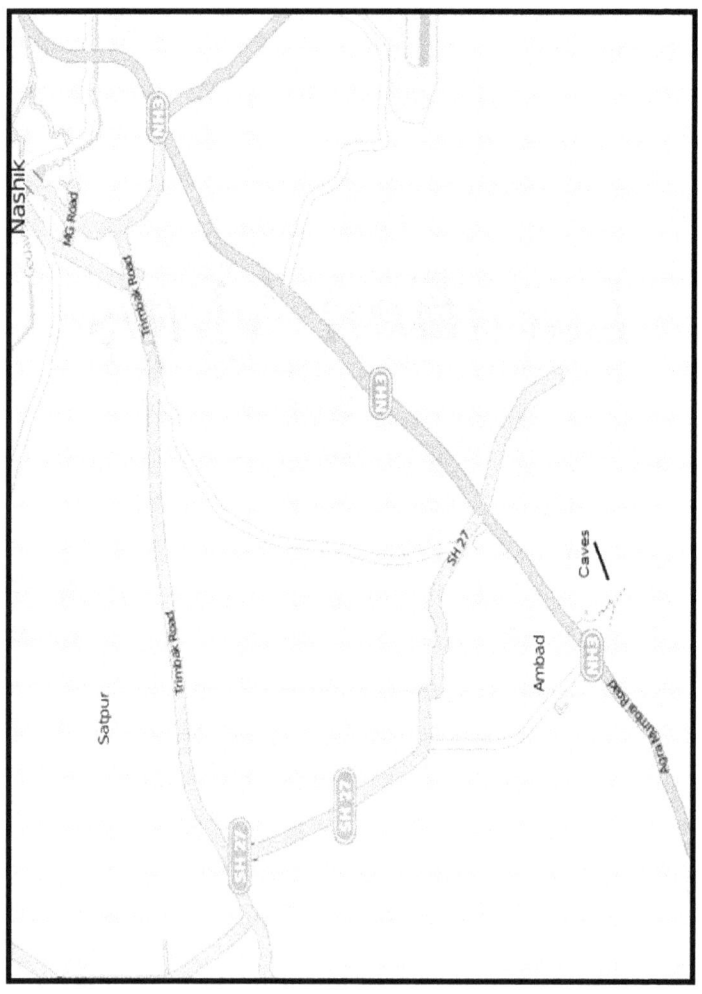

Map 2

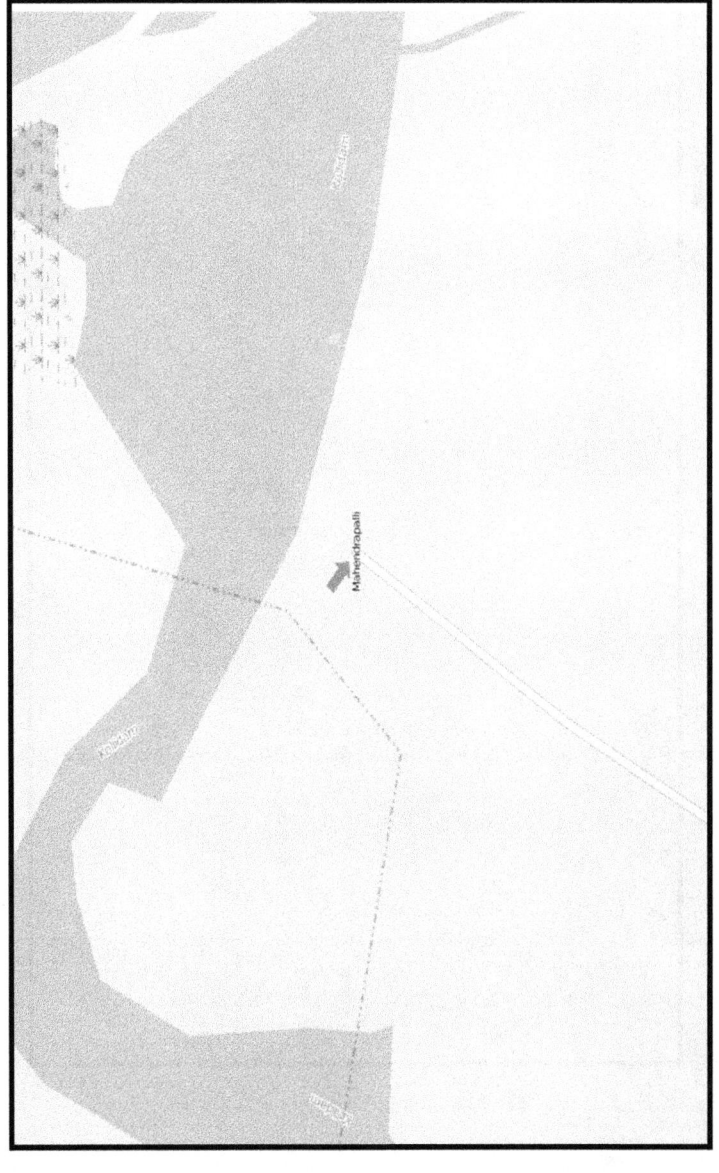

Map 3

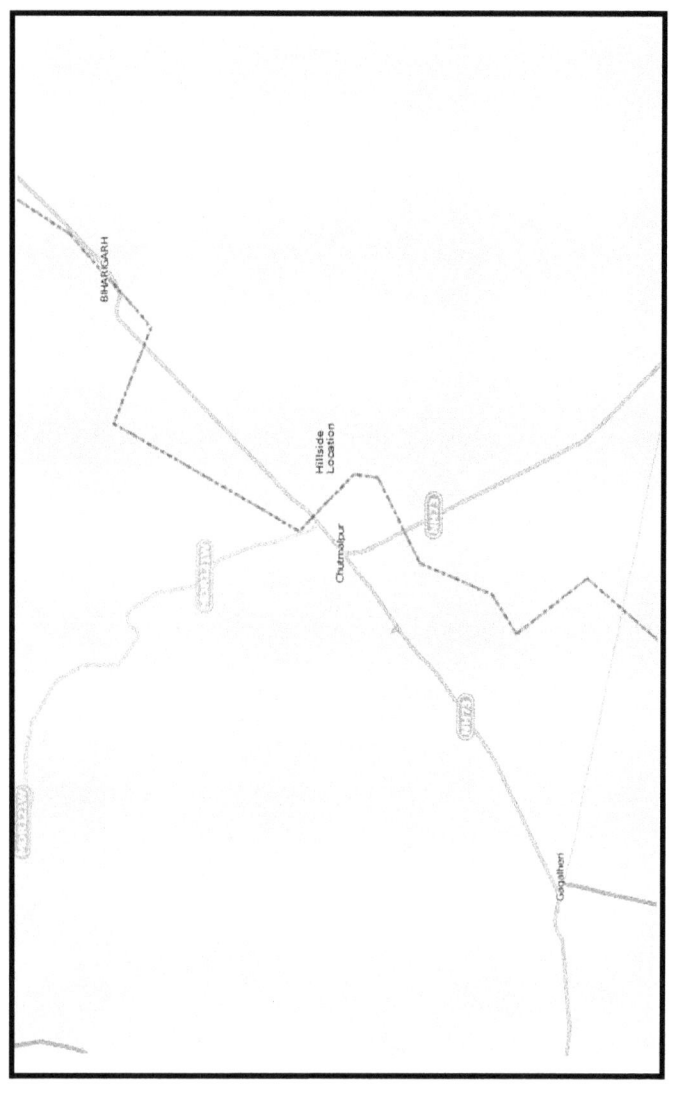

Map 4

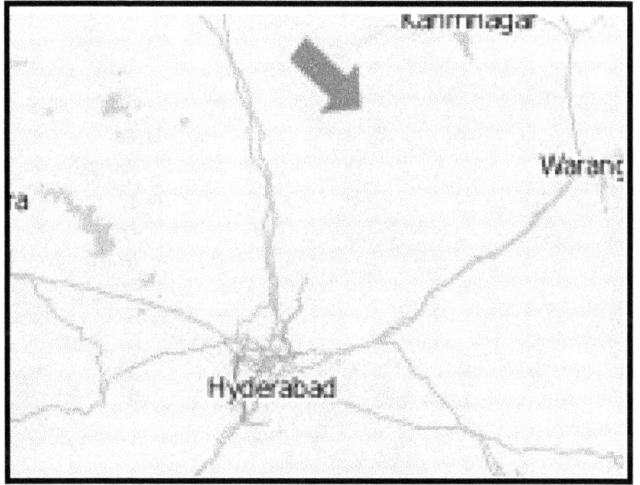

Yantra

Yantra Images

Yantra

Yantra

The following are Yantra images that have been scanned or photographed from actual Yantra's with the kind permission of the Tantric, or owners of the Yantra. For some Yantra permission was not given for photographing, or scanning, however some were allowed to be copied by hand and these are evident from the images.

The Yantra are referenced in Part 2 of this book (P.47).

Image 1

Image 2

Image 3

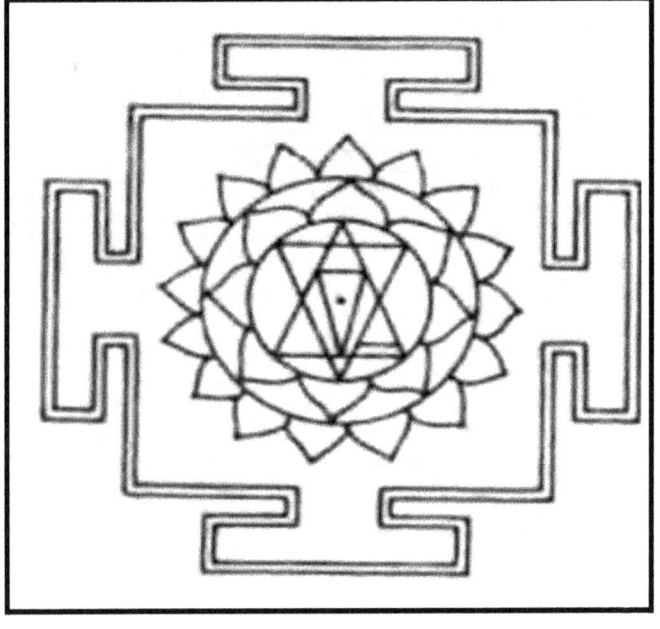

Image 4

Image 5

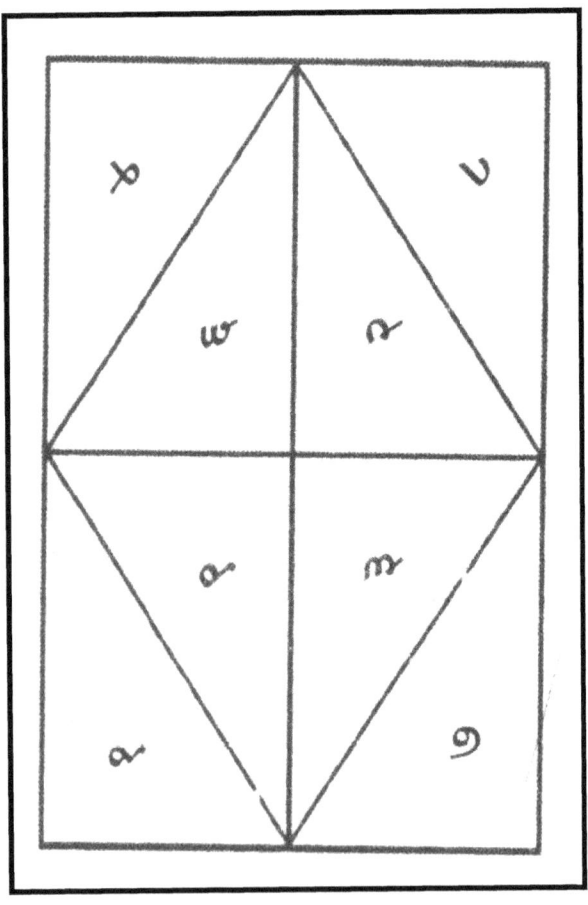

Image 6

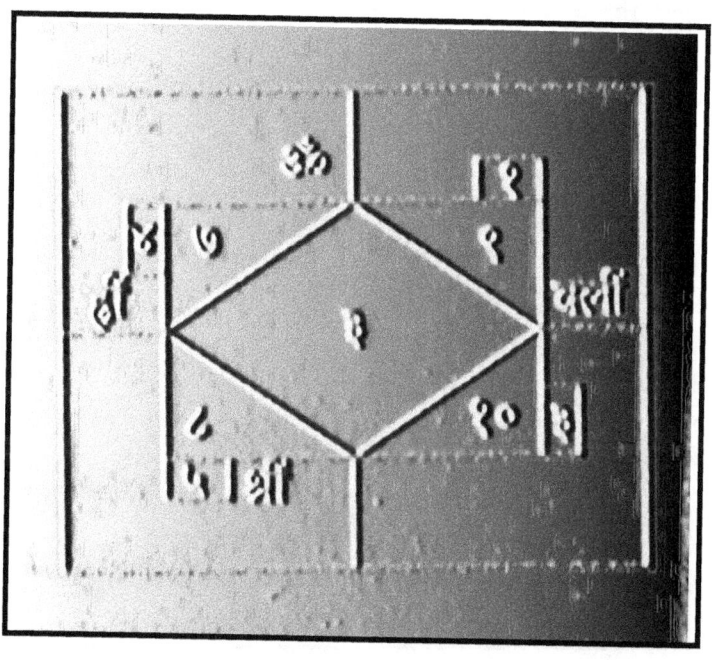

Image 7

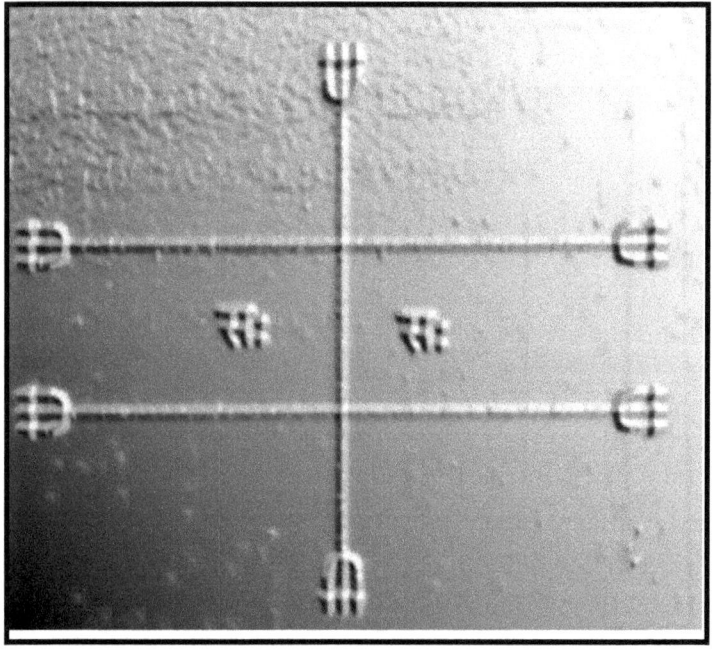

Image 8

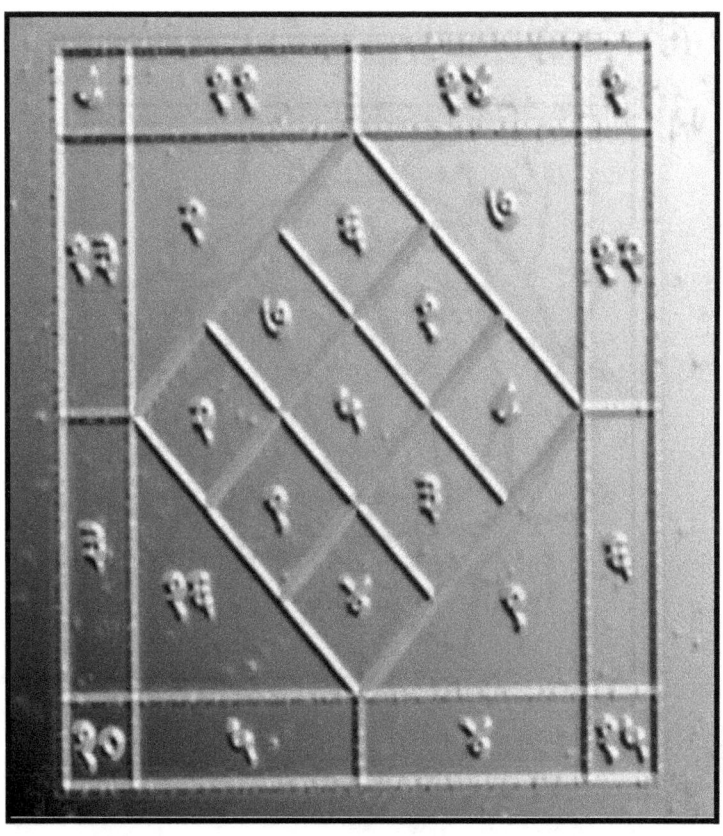

Image 9

Image 10

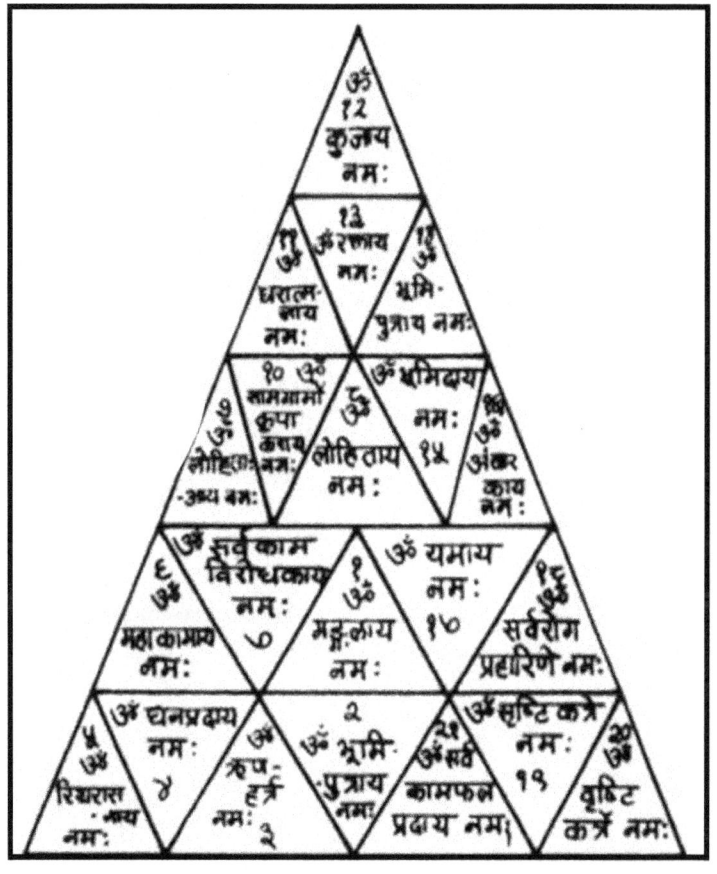

Image 11

Yantra

Image 12

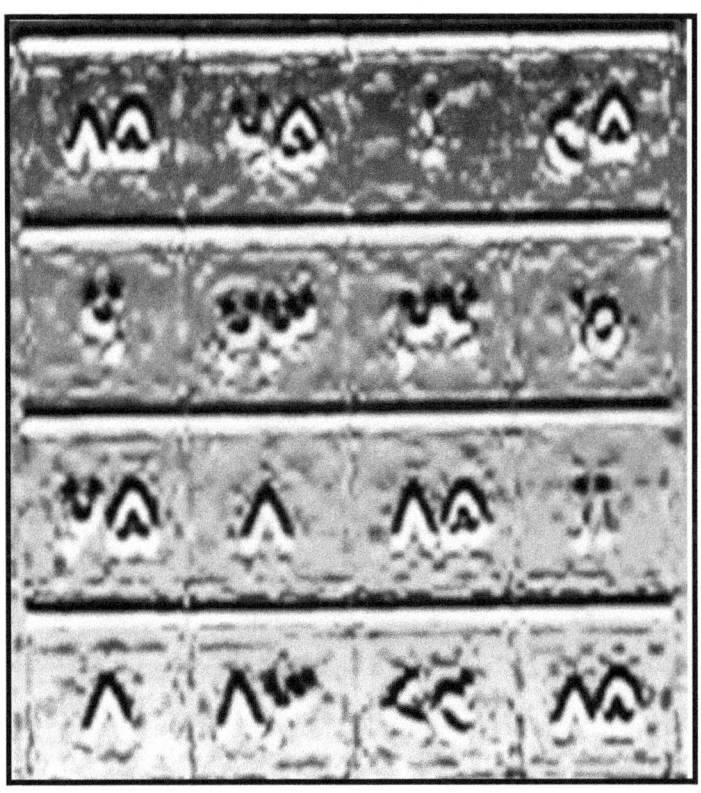

Image 13

Image 14

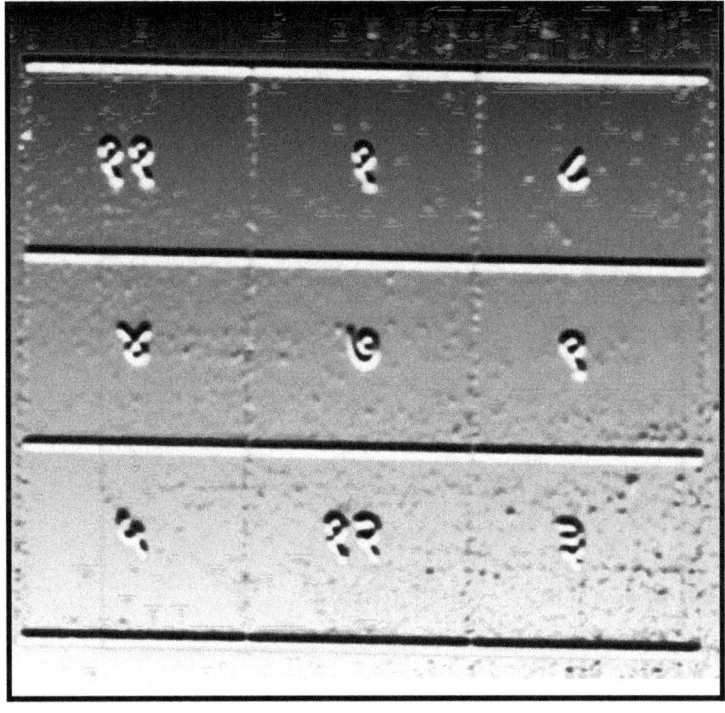

Image 15

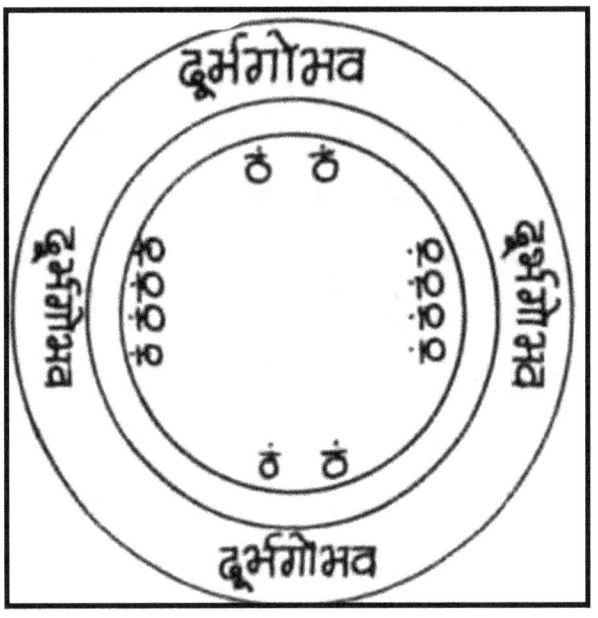

Image 16

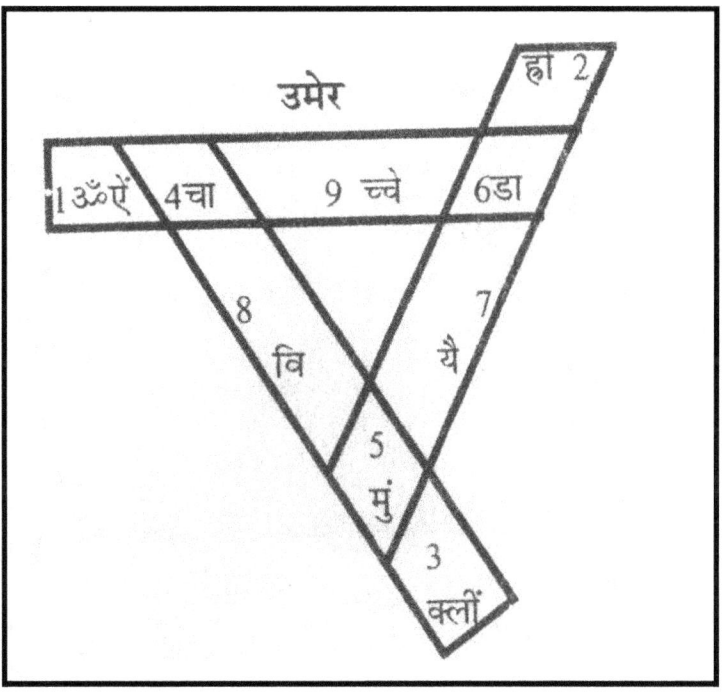

Image 17

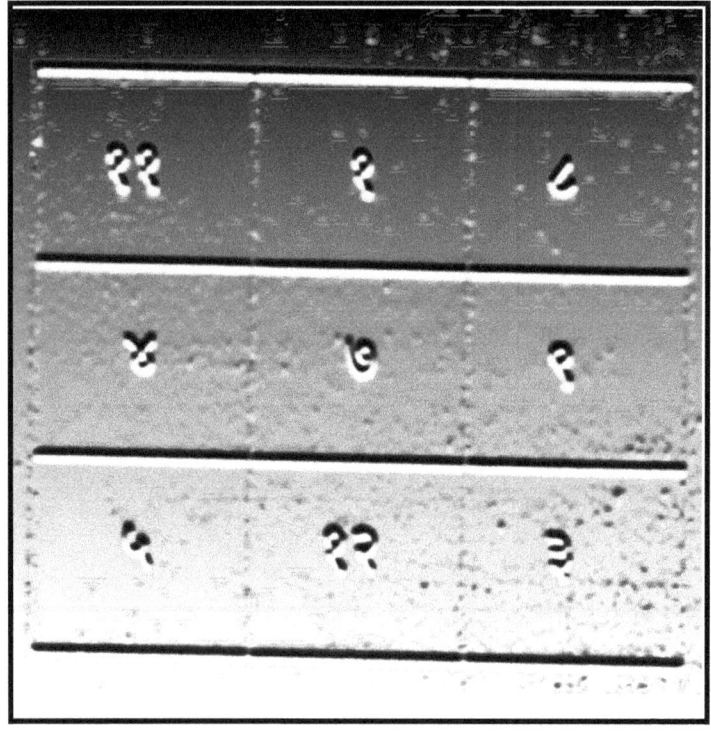

Image 18

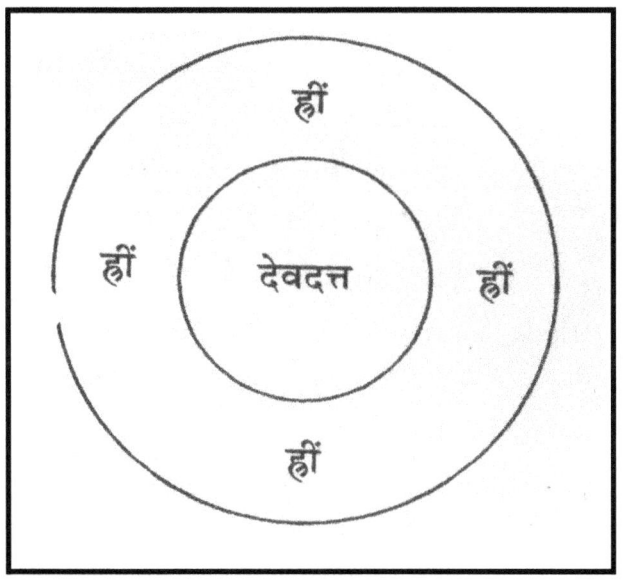

Image 19

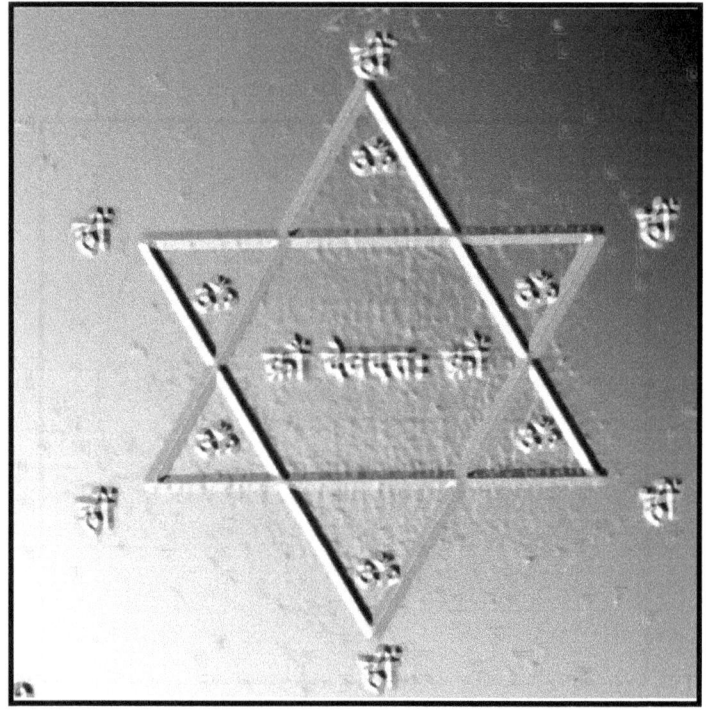

Image 20

Image 21

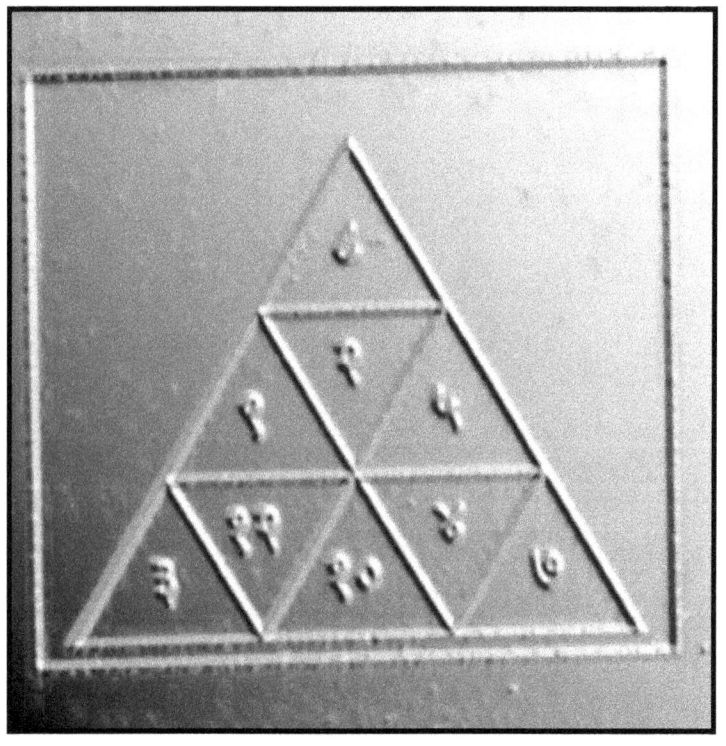

Yantra

Image 22

Image 23

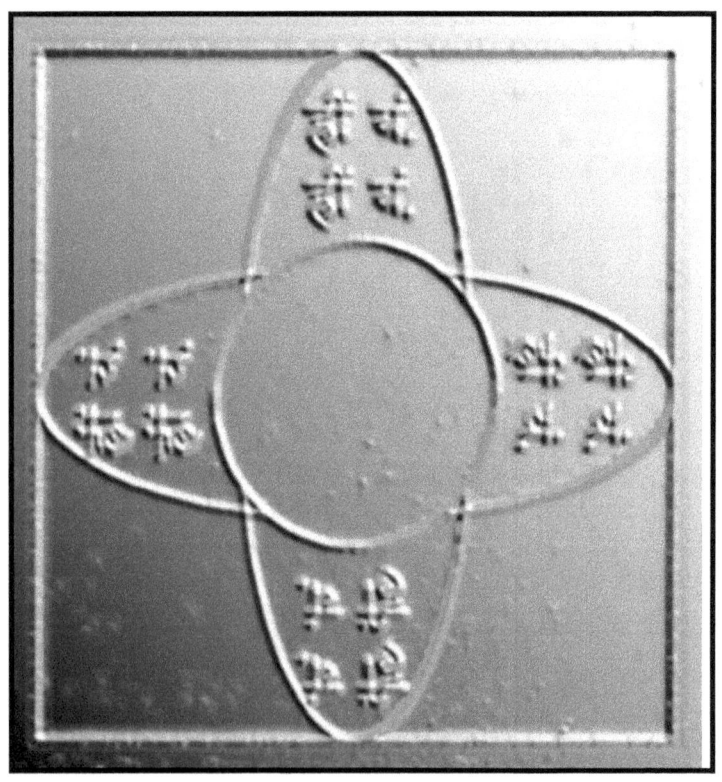

Image 24

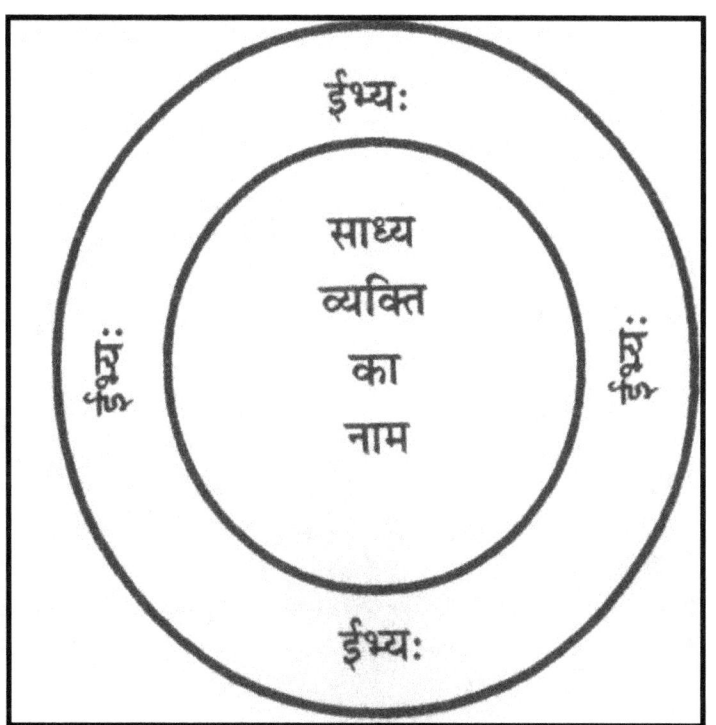

Image 25

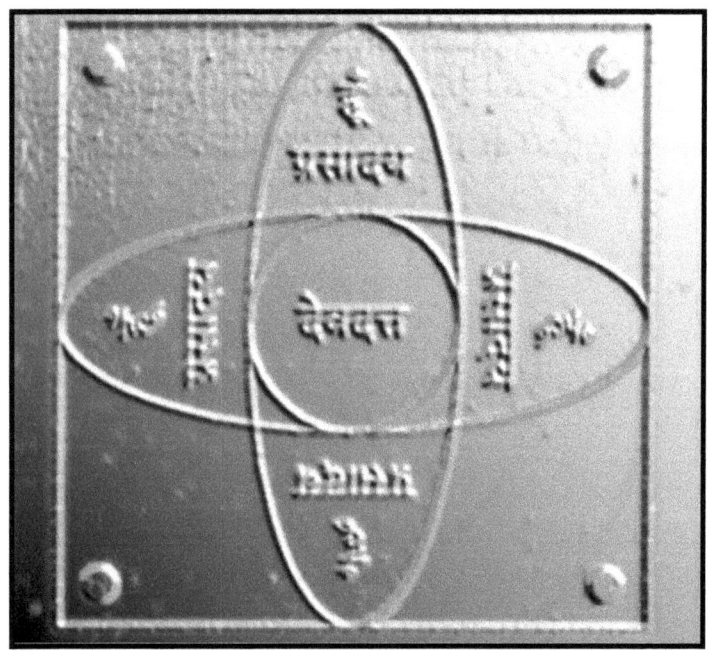

Yantra

Image 26

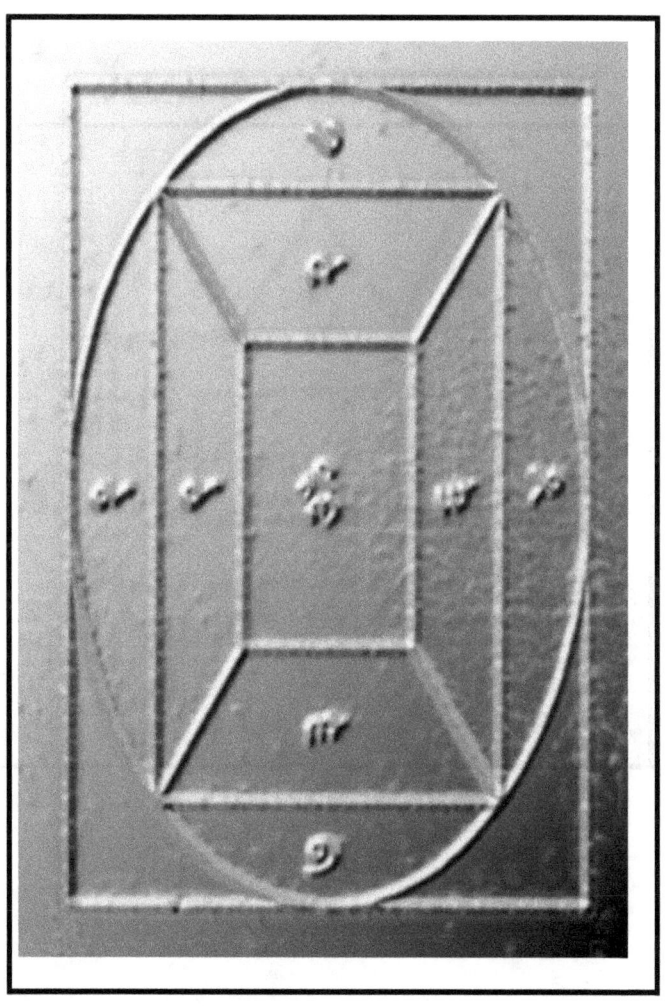

Image 27

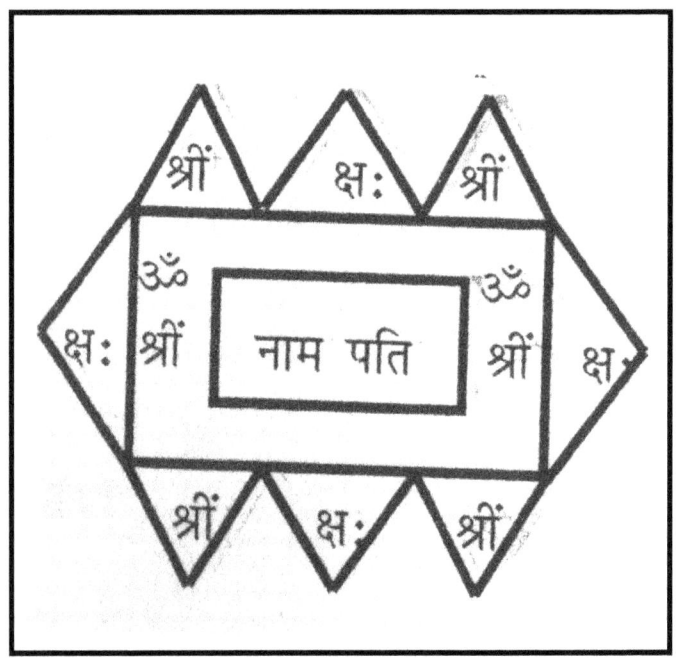

Image 28

Yantra

Image 29

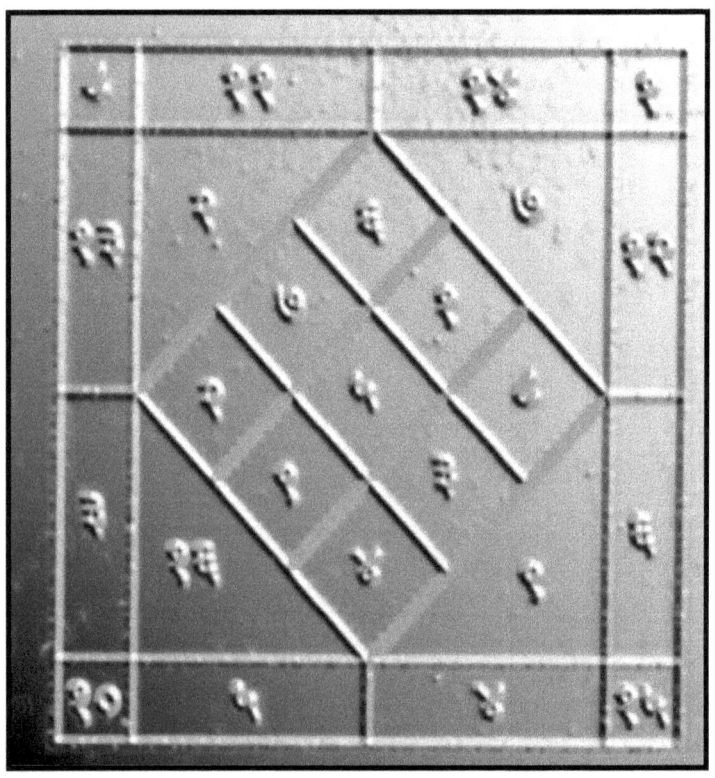

Image 30

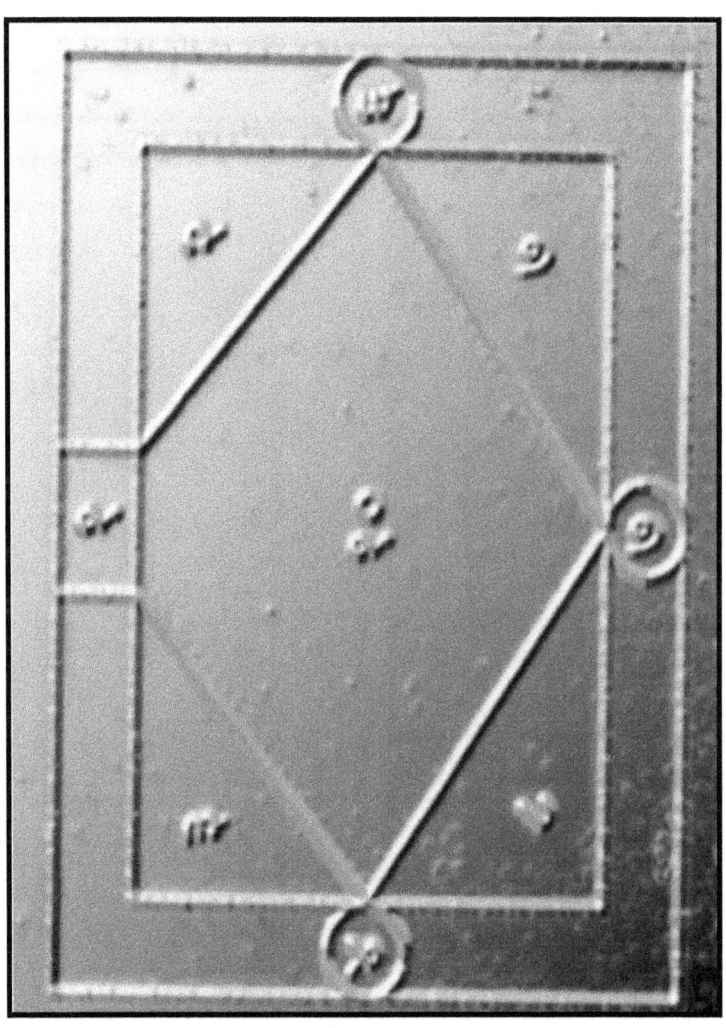

Image 31

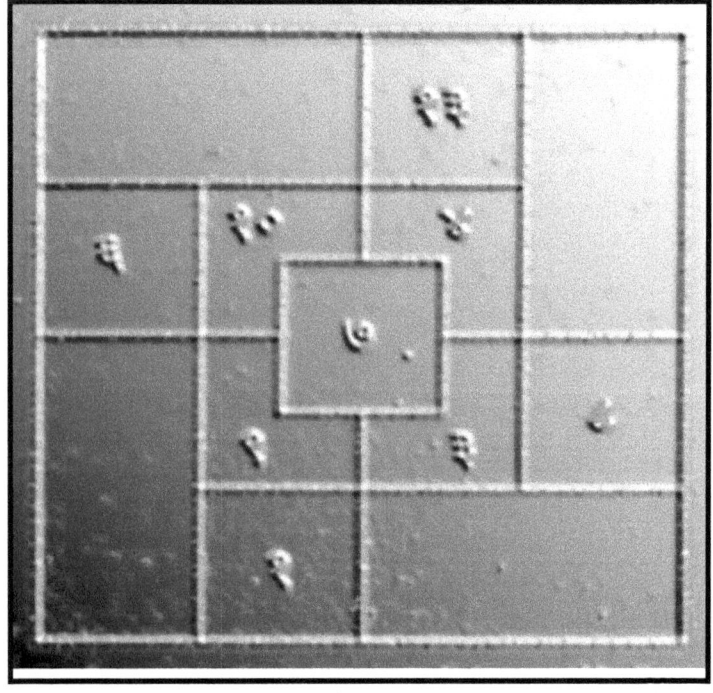

Yantra

Image 32

Image 33

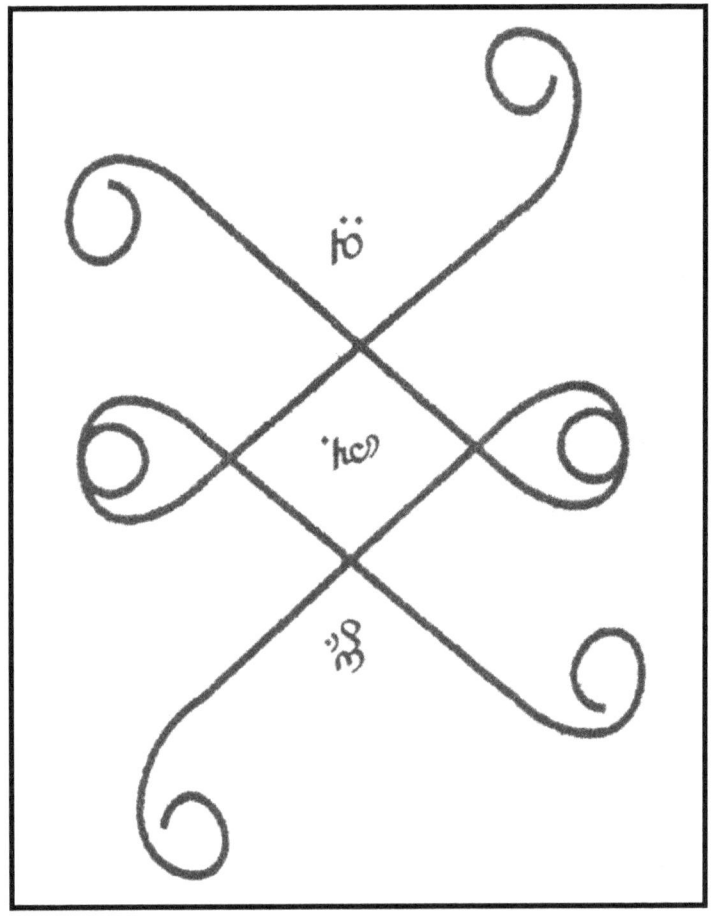

Image 34

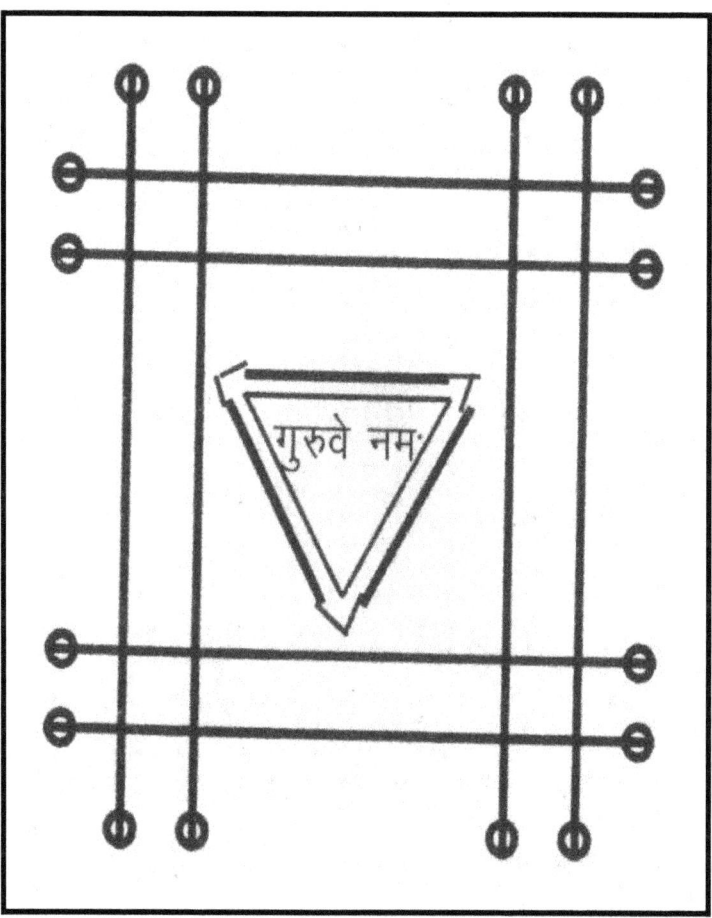

Image 35

Image 36

या हावज	३३३	३३७	३३१
या हावज	३२२	३३४	३३६
१९	३३७	३३०	३३५
कैदी का नाम मां का नाम	१९	या हावज	या हावज

Image 37

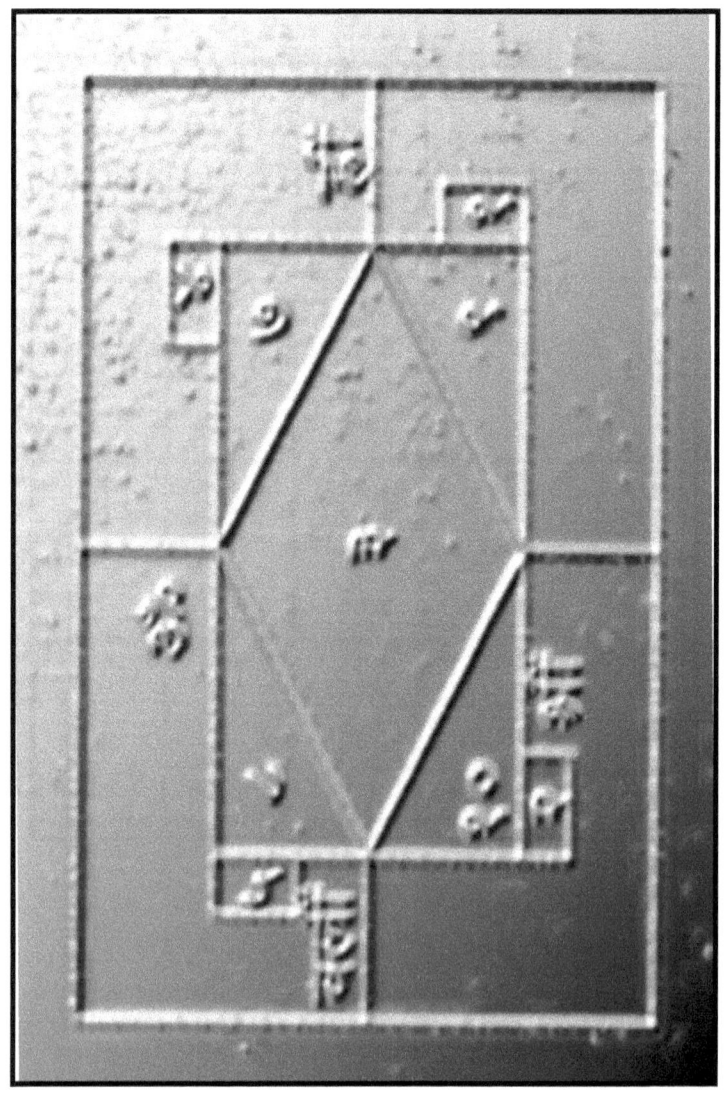

Yantra

Image 38

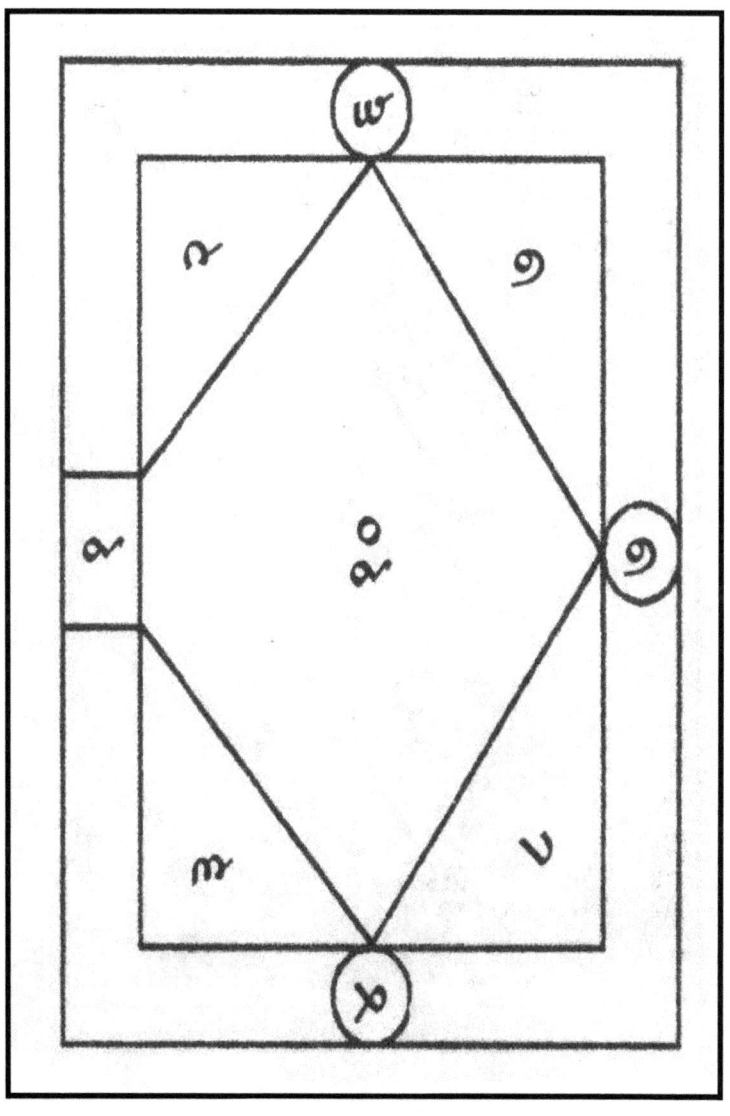

Image 39

Image 40

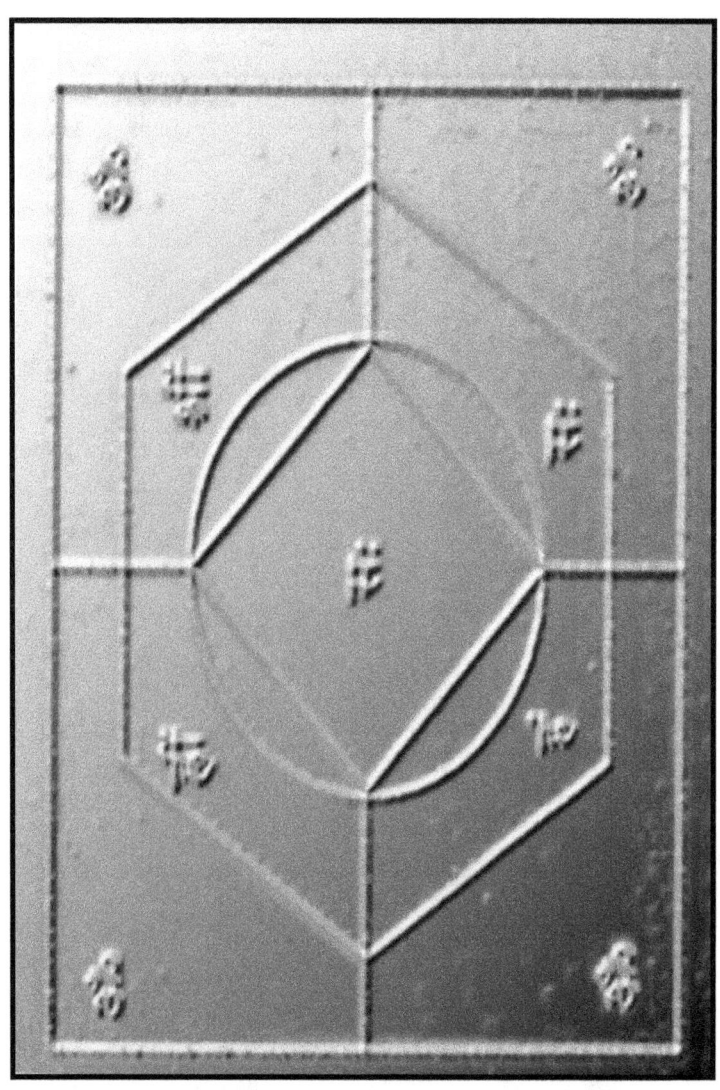

Image 41

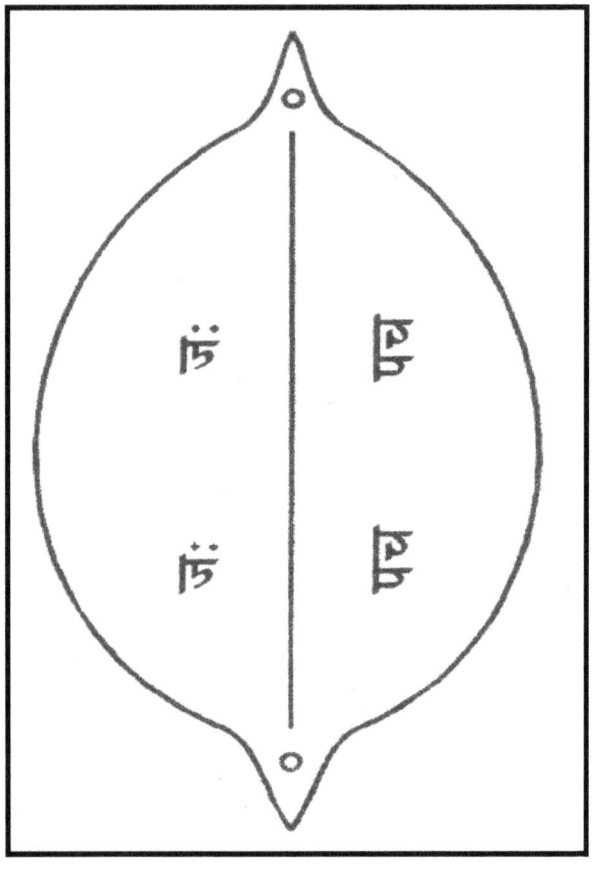

Image 42

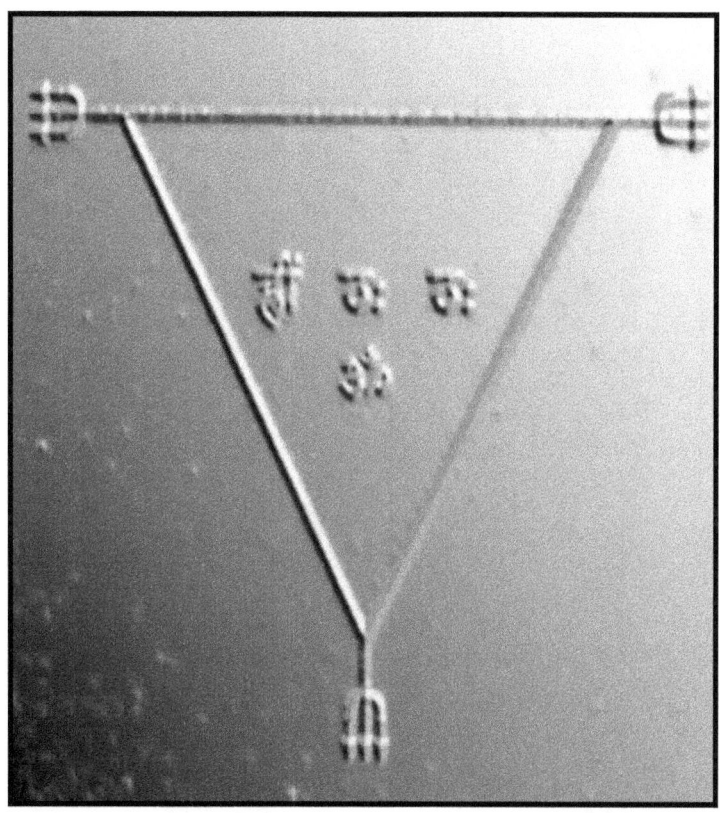

Yantra

References

Yantra

A

Algar, A, 1952. 'Translation Approaches to Sanskrit'. 3rd ed. London: Arcana Holdings.

Arnold, Edward A., ed 2009. 'As Long As Space Endures: Essays on the Kalacakra Tantra in Honor of H.H. the Dalai Lama'. Ithaca, NY: Snow Lion Publications.

Avalon, Arthur 1928. 'The Serpent Power'. Ganesh & Co..

B

Bagchi, P.C. 1986. 'Kaulajnana-nirnaya of the School of Matsyendranath'. Varanasi: Michael Magee, transl.

Bhattarchariya, K. 1962. 'Examining Vedic Manuscripts', Delhi: Khatary.

C

Charles, J. 1999 'Icons and Gods', Bombay: Neepalal.

Charlaine, M. 1984. 'Sound and Dimensional Awareness'. Paris. Degaulle Press

D

Davidson, Ronald M. 2003. 'Indian Esoteric Buddhism: A Social History of the Tantric Movement'. New York: Columbia University Press.

Davidson, Ronald M. 2005. 'Tibetan Renaissance: Tantric Buddhism in the Rebirth of Tibetan Culture'. New York: Columbia University Press. .

E

Edward, Paul. 1990 'Ancient Metallurgy': London. Friar.

Esteban, P. 2001. 'Le Sanskrit' Paris. Jean Paul Press.

F

Feuerstein, Georg. 1998. 'Tantra: The Path of Ecstasy'. Boston: Shambhala.

Fran, E. 'Ayurveda: A study'. Florida. New Age Solutions.

G

Guenon, Rene 2004. 'Studies in Hinduism: Collected Works' (2nd ed.). Sophia Perennis.

Gyatso, Geshe Kelsang 2003. 'Tantric Grounds and Paths'. Tharpa Publications.

Gyatso, Geshe Kelsang 2005. 'Mahamudra Tantra'. Tharpa Publications.

Gyatso, Tenzin; Tsong-ka-pa, Jeffrey Hopkins 1987. 'Deity Yoga'. Ithaca, NY: Snow Lion Publications.

Gokulala Mirabhai, M. P., 1950. 'Theory of Sanskruti Practice'. 1st ed. Lucknow: Neem press.

Gurdut, M. P. 1955. 'Dialects if the Ancients'. 1st ed. Lucknow: Neem press.

H

Harrison, R, 1940. 'A Treatise on Sanskrit of the Hindustani' 1st ed. Calcutta: Orthtello Press.

Harold, P.J. 1991. 'The Resonant Brain'. Delhi. Mahendra.

I

Indam, D, 1955. 'Finding methods in Sanskrit Calculus'. 3rd ed. London: Neasden Press.

Indira, L. 1993. 'Masonary Spectral Anlaysis of Indian Temples', Bangalore: Ananda.

K

Kane, Pandurang Vaman. 2001, 'History of Dharmashastra' Pune: Bhandarkar Oriental Research Institute.

Keiffe, Lauren. 1990 'Hidden Meanings in Hinduism'. Dawn Press

L

Lorna, L. 1953. Ancient Hinduism, Bangalore: Ananda.

Lorimer, Jean. 1988. Metal Alchemy, Lahore press.

M

Magee, Michael, tr. 1984. 'Yoni Tantra'. Madras. Ahora.

Mahendranath, Shri Gurudev 2001. 'The Scrolls of Mahendranath'. Seattle: International Nath Order.

McDaniel, June. 2004. 'Offering Flowers, Feeding Skulls: Popular Goddess Worship in West Bengal'. New York: Oxford University Press.

Mookerji, Ajit 1997. 'The Tantric Way: Art, Science, Ritual'. London: Thames & Hudson.

N

Nesbitt, K. 1962. 'Thugee: Lives', Delhi: Gorilal Press.

Nafiza, Iqbal. 1977 'Sanskrit Interpretations': Lahore Press

Nadeem, I 2001. 'Last Rites' California. Abraham ltd.

O

O' Neil, K. 1948 'Tantriks of Indian Life', Delhi: Gorilal Press.

O' Keiffe, M. 1987. 'Meta-States and Transdimentional Spaces', Cambridge. Dawn.

P

Palmer, P, 1944. 'Ancient Texts'. 1st ed. Bombay: Queens.

Polanski, P. 1985. 'Developmental Approach to Ancient Languages', Thema Langua, 9(1).

Q

Quinn, R, 1949. Living the Indian Way. 1st ed. Bombay: Queens, S. 1999. 'Vedic Shaminism'. Edinburgh. McTavish Press

R

Rao, T. A. Gopinatha 1981. 'Elements in Hindu Iconography'. Madras: Law Printing House.

Rogers, L. 1988. 'Changes in Translational Techniques', Translation World, 3(7).

S

Shawn, C. 1994 'Integration and Semantics',Oxford: Peterloo.

Singh, D. 1974 'Temple Constructions', Bangalore: Ananda.

Singh, K. 1982 'Ancient Buildings and No Cement', Construction International, 4(2).

Smith, Frederick M. 2006. 'The Self Possessed: Deity and Spirit Possession in South Asian Literature'. Columbia University Press, USA.

Swann, J. 2002 'Textual Extraction Techniques',Oxford: Synestry.

T

Thomas, Kenneth. 1960. 'Brain States', Oxford Press

Than, Kier. 1978. Transformation and Tantrism. 2nd ed. Sweden. Sneha.

U

Urban, Hugh. 2002 'The Conservative Character of Tantra: Secrecy, Sacrifice and This-Worldly Power in Bengali Śākta Tantra'. International Journal of Tantric Studies 6 (1).

W

Walker, Benjamin. 1982. 'Tantrism: Its Secret Principles and Practices'. London:Acquarian Press.

Wallis, Glenn. 2002. 'Mediating the Power of Buddhas: Ritual in the Mañjuśrīmūlakalpa'. Albany: State University of New York Press.

White, David Gordon. 2003. 'Kiss of the Yogini: 'Tantric Sex' in its South Asian Contexts. Chicago: University of Chicago Press.

White, David Gordon. 1998. 'The Alchemical Body: Siddha Traditions in Medieval India'. Chicago: University of Chicago Press.

Woodroffe, John. 1913. 'Mahanirvana Tantra: Tantra of the Great Liberation 'Arthur Avalon, transl.

Appendix:
Websites

Yantra

The following websites scored highly based on a detailed rating scale.

Agni-hotri Suppliers
http://www.agno_hotri.medalian.com

Real Yantra
http://www.realyantra.com

Ram-das & Sons
http://www.ram.jevani.ind.com

Rudraksha and Samigri (due to be relaunched in 2013)
http://www.rs.samagri.com

Yantra

Final Word

The compilation of this work has been a long and exhaustive process and could not have been completed without the help and assistance of all those involved. It is hoped the information in this book will reaffirm the significance of ancient vedic texts, and also highlight the power of Yantra. The work will also provide a way forward to tackle the question often posed by those who take a skeptical stance, as to why Yantra's do not work, or have limited effect. This work has provided sufficient infomation to illiustrate the rareity of genuine Yantra, and provided a way forward to obtaining Yantra if people so wish. More importantly I hope this work will bring a greater appreciation of Vedic knowledge and lead people to discover further the vast body of Vedic works. For the future I have been asked to assist with other research in to other Vedic texts, some of which came about from the work that started with this book. There was also some material which was beyond the scope of this work which related to practical applications of Vedic knowledge. Although there is already a large body of work regarding this, there is I believe, a lot which has not been discovered, or explained sufficently for the layperson to put into practice. There is a blog which I try to maintain as best as I can with regard to my time commitments. Although the blog relates to my first book, I do mention current and future works in progress.

Comments are also welcome on the blog and I am able to respond to them, be they general comments or specific questions.

The blog address is: http://listpower.blogspot.com/

Feedback is welcome, and can be done so by contacting the publishers directly by email: admin@neepradaka.co.uk

Yantra

www.ingramcontent.com/pod-product-compliance
Lightning Source LLC
Chambersburg PA
CBHW051925160426
43198CB00012B/2046